50 Shades of Stitches

Popular Ribbing

Knitting Patterns with Step-by-Step Instructions

Printed in the United States of America First Printing, 2019

ISBN **978-1-63227-099-3**

SCR MEDIA Inc.

Box 7103

Delray Beach Fl. 33482

561-909-6975

*If you enjoyed this book and found some benefit in reading this, I'd like to hear from you and hope that you could take some time to post a review on Amazon. Your feedback and support will help this author to improve her writing craft significantly for future projects and make this book even better. Just type this link into your web browser **Getbook.at/Vol1** or scan the code below*

QR CODE

Table of Contents

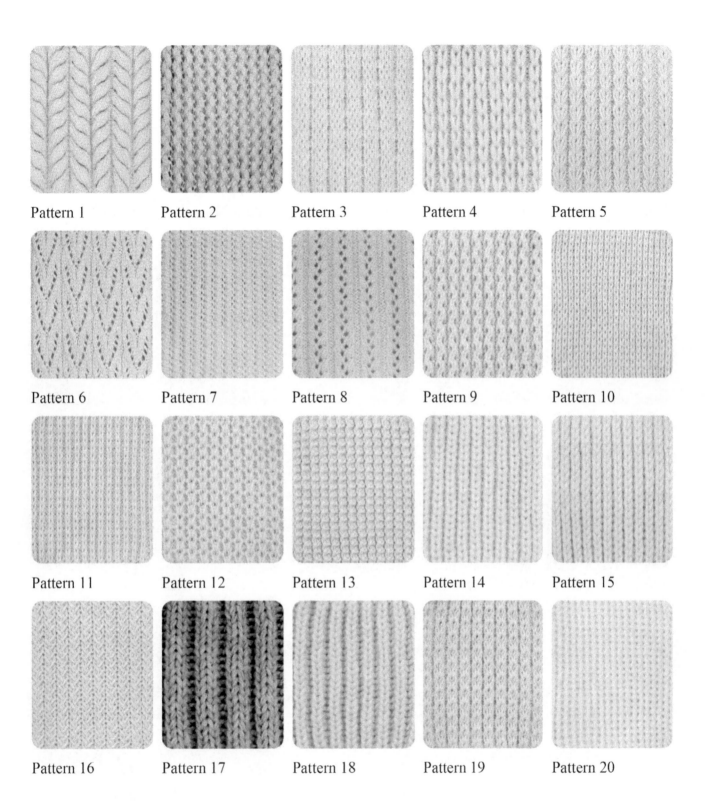

Pattern 1   Pattern 2   Pattern 3   Pattern 4   Pattern 5

Pattern 6   Pattern 7   Pattern 8   Pattern 9   Pattern 10

Pattern 11   Pattern 12   Pattern 13   Pattern 14   Pattern 15

Pattern 16   Pattern 17   Pattern 18   Pattern 19   Pattern 20

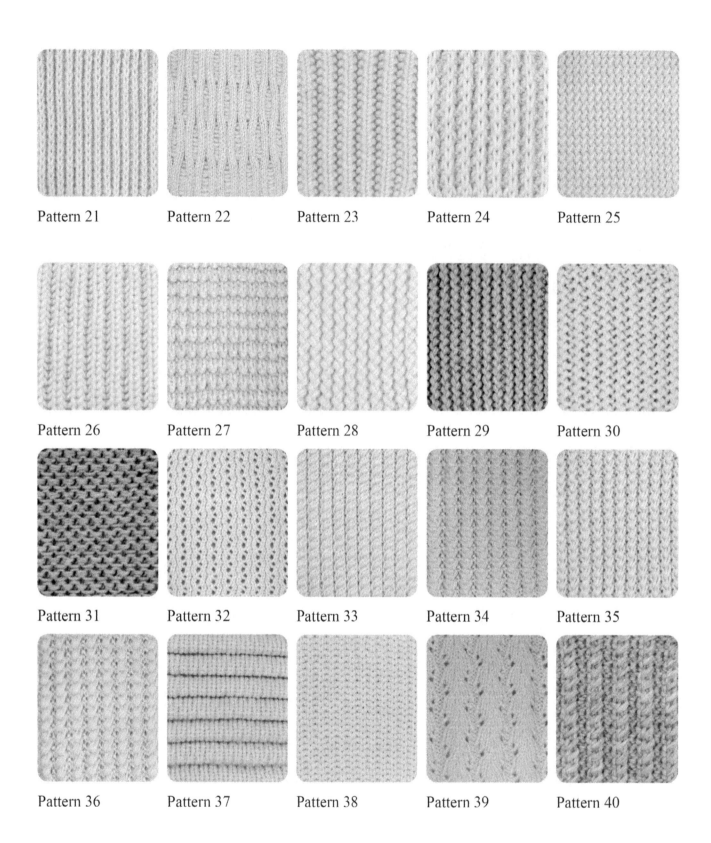

Pattern 21   Pattern 22   Pattern 23   Pattern 24   Pattern 25

Pattern 26   Pattern 27   Pattern 28   Pattern 29   Pattern 30

Pattern 31   Pattern 32   Pattern 33   Pattern 34   Pattern 35

Pattern 36   Pattern 37   Pattern 38   Pattern 39   Pattern 40

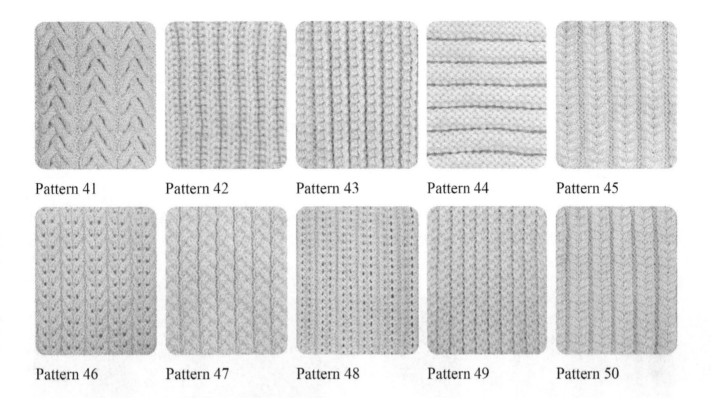

Pattern 41   Pattern 42   Pattern 43   Pattern 44   Pattern 45

Pattern 46   Pattern 47   Pattern 48   Pattern 49   Pattern 50

Get a Free Bonus

3 More Knitting Patterns

Would you like 3 more knitting patterns? Download your 3 free knitting patterns at https://BookHip.com/BXBSBJH

Introduction

Alternating knit and purl stitches in various combinations create ribs, which are very popular due to their simplicity and stretchy, voluminous texture. There are two types: simple ribs, which consist of alternating knit and purl stitches, and decorative ones, which include other elements of knitting such as yarn overs, slipped stitches, elongated stitches, and twisted stitches.

Simple ribs have steady names such as 1x1, 2x2, 3x3, and the like, which indicate the numbers of alternating knit and purl stitches. The first digit indicates the number of knit stitches, and the second digit indicates the number of purl stitches. Decorative ribbed patterns usually have various fancy and intricate names.

The names of numbered ribbed patterns are always the same, whereas decorative ones' names may vary. The same decorative pattern can have several names, or different patterns can have the same name. Since most decorative patterns do not have steady names, they will be unnamed in this book, letting knitters call them as they like.

Ribbing is almost an essential element of knitting. It is used to prevent the edges from curling up. Ribbing is also frequently used as decorative patterns. We recommend knitting ribs tightly and through the back legs. It reduces their tendency to stretch, as the knit fabric will keep the shape better. Tight knitting works well in combination with knitting through the back legs, which is the second knitting way.

For beginning knitters, we would like to say that there are two ways of knitting stitches. The first way, most common, creates a plain loop by knitting through the stitch's front leg, which the stitch's leg closest to the front side. The second knitting method is knitting through the stitch's back leg, closest to the backside. In this book, for clarity, we call the first—conventional—way "knitting through the front leg" and the second way of knitting "knitting through the back leg." Purl stitches of the first and second knitting methods are also worked differently (see recommendations below).

Despite the rules, the method of knitting stitches is a matter of habit and preference, and many knitters prefer the second way, i.e., knitting through the back leg, as many patterns come out well both ways. Sometimes, however, patterns require a specific way of knitting stitches—through the front legs or the back legs or a combination of both—and incorrect turns of the stitches can distort, significantly change, or completely ruin the design of the pattern.

Some knitters tend to mix the first and second knitting methods (i.e., knitting through the front leg and knitting through the back leg), using knit stitches of the first method and purl stitches of the second one. This mix, however, affects the evenness of stitches, and as a result, it affects the texture of the knit fabric.

Ribbed patterns, in particular, are better to knit the second way, working both knit and purl stitches this way. When a ribbed pattern is knitted the second way, it stretches less, holds the shape better, and has a more tight texture. However, some ribbed patterns, especially braids and cables with frequent intersections, are better to knit conventionally, i.e., through the front legs, to add some softness to frequently intersected stitches.

Twisted stitches are a particular method of knitting. These stitches, as regular ones, can be worked two ways. The first way of working twisted stitches is based on knitting through the front legs, and the second way of working twisted stitches is based on knitting through the back legs. Let's look at both ways.

In the first way of twisted knitting, the knit stitch works through the back leg, instead of the front leg, as usual, and the purl stitch works through the back leg, instead of the front leg, as usual. However, the purl stitch works the same way as if to purl in regular knitting through the front leg, when the knit stitch sets up to be knitted through the front leg—thus, the stitch becomes twisted. The stitches of the first way are less twisted, less tight, and come out more even.

In the second way of twisted knitting, the front leg of the knit stitch moves to the back, inserting the right needle through the back leg from back to front and slipping it onto the right needle, then inserting the left needle through this slipped stitch from left to right and slipping it from the right needle to the left one. Then this stitch knits through the back leg (i.e., through the former front leg). The purl stitch works through the back leg, instead of the front leg, as usual, as if to purl in regular knitting through the back leg when the knit stitch sets up for knitting through the back leg. The second way's stitches are tighter as they are more twisted and because they are based on regular knitting through the back legs, which is tighter than knitting through the front legs.

Twisted stitches are an element of decorative knitting. They are smaller and tighter than regular stitches and look like tiny braids. These stitches are frequently used in complicated Japanese knitting patterns. In regular knitting, twisted stitches can be used for trimming, in ribbing 1x1 or 2x2, various tiny braids and cables, and the like.

As we can see, all ways of knitting stitches are essential and have a purpose. Whatever way you prefer to knit for a particular pattern, just remember that stitches knitted correctly improve your knit's quality.

— Marina Molo

Recommendations

Two Ways of Knitting Stitches

Knitting through the front leg: Knit through the front leg, inserting the right needle through the stitch from left to right; purl as follows: with the working yarn in front of the stitch, insert the right needle through the stitch from back to front and wrap the working yarn forward (i.e., from yourself) around the tip of the right needle, then pull the working yarn with the right needle through the stitch. **Note:** The purl stitch that is worked this way sets up the knit stitch to be knitted through the front leg. This method of knitting is the most popular and known as conventional.

Knitting through the back leg: Knit through the back leg, inserting the right needle through the stitch from front to back; purl as follows: with the working yarn in front of the stitch, insert the right needle through the stitch from back to front, move the working yarn under the right needle, and pull it with the needle through the stitch. **Note:** The purl stitch that is worked this way sets up the knit stitch to be knitted through the back leg.

How to Do Yarn Over

Unless indicated otherwise, the working yarn goes from the needle's front towards the back when the knit stitch follows a yarn over. In this case, the description reads "yarn over forward (i.e., from yourself)." When the purl stitch follows a yarn over, the working yarn goes from behind the needle towards the front. In this case, the description reads "yarn over backward (i.e., to yourself)."

How to Work the Edge Stitches

The first way: Slip the first edge stitch; purl the last edge stitch as if to purl in knitting through back leg as follows: with the working yarn in front of the stitch, insert the right needle through the stitch from back to front, then move the working yarn under the right needle and pull it with the needle through the stitch. Note: Regardless of the method of knitting, through the front legs or the back legs, purl the last edge stitch as if to purl in knitting through the back leg, as this way of working the last edge stitch creates more tight and even edges.

The second way: Knit both the first edge stitch and the last edge stitch through the front leg (or, depending on the pattern, through the back legs). Note: This way of working the edge stitches is used in patterns in which otherwise the left edge comes out loose and slightly stretchy. This way of knitting the edge stitches creates even edges on both sides.

How to Bind off Ribbed Stitches

The first method: Slip the edge stitch onto the right needle, knit 1 (or purl 1), then insert the left needle through the slipped edge stitch from left to right and pass it over the knitted (or purled) stitch, *now there is 1 stitch on the right needle, knit (or purl) the next stitch (now there are 2 stitches on the right needle), insert the left needle through the 1ˢᵗ stitch on the right needle from left to right and pass it over the 2ⁿᵈ stitch* repeat from * to * until the end of the row.

The second method: Unless instructed otherwise, after the last row on the Front Side, turn your work over. Back Side: Slip all stitches from the left needle to the right one; thus, the working yarn is at the end of the row; turn your work over. Front Side: Slip 2 stitches purlwise from the left needle to the right one, insert the left needle through the front leg of the 1ˢᵗ slipped stitch from left to right, and pass it over the 2ⁿᵈ stitch (now there is 1 stitch on the right needle) *slip 1 stitch purlwise from the left needle to the right one, insert the left needle through the front leg of the 1ˢᵗ stitch on the right needle from left to right and pass it over the 2ⁿᵈ stitch, now there is 1 stitch on the right needle* repeat from * to * until the end of the row.

Note: This method of binding off creates a tight chain of stitches that may not require finishing. For trimming, knit the last row and bind off using larger needles than the working ones to create larger edge stitches.

Pattern 1

Cast on a multiple of 3. Knit without the edge stitches. Three-stitch repeat. Repeat rows: 3-11. **Knit through the back leg, purl as follows:** With the working yarn in front of the stitch, insert the right needle through the stitch from back to front, move the working yarn under the right needle, and pull it with the needle through the stitch. **Note:** The purl stitch that is worked this way sets up the knit stitch to be knitted through the back leg.

Note: This pattern knits differently: The width knits vertically. Cast on the number of stitches required for the height of your work. Knit the required width vertically, and then turn your work horizontally. **Knit tightly. Needles: U.S. no. 4 (3.5 mm).**

Description:

Row 1: Slip 1, knit all the stitches.

Row 2: Slip 1, purl all the stitches.

Row 3: Knit 6 stitches as follows: *Slip 1 purlwise, knit 5, then, leaving the rest of the stitches on the left needle, turn your work over to the Back Side. **The Back Side:** Slip 1 purlwise, purl 5, turn your work over to the Front Side* repeat from * to * 5 more times. **The Front Side:** Slip 1, knit 8, then, leaving the rest of the stitches on the left needle, turn your work over to the Back Side. **The Back Side:** Slip 1, purl 5, then, leaving 3 stitches on the left needle, turn your work over to the Front Side. **The Front Side:** ***Slip 1, knit 5, then turn your work over to the Back Side. **The Back Side:** Slip 1, purl 5, then turn your work over to the Front Side* repeat from *** to * 4 more times, then—on **the Front Side**—slip 1, knit 8, then turn your work over to the Back Side. **The Back Side:** Slip 1 purlwise, purl 5, then, leaving 3 more stitches on the left needle, turn your work over to the Front Side*** Repeat from *** to *** until the end of the row, until the last 6 stitches. **The Front Side:** Knit the last 6 stitches as follows: ****Slip 1, knit 5, then turn your work over to the Back Side. **The Back Side:** Slip 1, purl 5**** repeat from **** to **** 4 more times (i.e., 8 rows). The last row: purl all the stitches until the end of the row, connecting the separately knitted stitches in this row.

Row 4 (Front Side): For the design of this pattern, bind off all the stitches as follows: *knit 2 together through the back legs, then slip the received stitch from the right needle to the left one* repeat from * to * until the end of the row.

Row 5 (Back Side): Cast on **the same number of stitches** from the chain of bound off stitches as follows: *With the working yarn in front of the needle, pick up the back leg of each bound off stitch onto the right needle, inserting the needle from back to front, then move the working yarn under the needle and push it back through the stitch* repeat from * to * until the end of the row.

Row 6 (Front Side): Slip 1, knit all the stitches.

Row 7 (Back Side): Note: From row 7, start knitting on the Back Side as follows: *Slip 1, purl 5, then, leaving the rest of the stitches on the left needle, turn your work over to the Front Side. **The Front Side:** Slip 1, knit 5, then turn your work over to the Back Side* repeat from * to * 5 more times, then—on **the Back Side**—slip 1, purl 8, then, leaving the rest of the stitches on the left needle, turn your work over to the Front Side. **The Front Side:** Slip 1, knit 5, then, leaving 3 stitches on the left needle, turn your work over to the Back Side. **The Back Side:** ***Slip 1, purl 5, then turn your work over to the Front Side. **The Front Side:** Slip 1, knit 5, then turn your work over to the Back Side* repeat from *** to * 4 more times (i.e., 8 rows), then—on **the Back Side**—slip 1, purl 8, turn your work over to the Front Side. **The Front Side:** Slip 1, knit 5, then, leaving 3 more stitches on the left needle, turn your work over to the Back Side*** Repeat from *** to *** until the end of the row, until the last 6 stitches. **The Back Side.** Purl the last 6 stitches as follows: ****Slip 1, purl 5, then turn your work over to the Front Side. **The Front Side:** Slip 1, knit 5, then turn your work over to the Back Side**** repeat from **** to **** 3 more times (i.e., 6 rows). **The Back Side:** Slip 1, purl 5, then turn your work over to the Front Side.

Row 8 (Front Side): Slip 1, knit all the stitches, connecting the separately knitted stitches in this row.

Row 9 (Back Side): For the design of this pattern, bind off all the stitches purlwise as follows: *purl 2 together as if to purl in knitting through the back legs: with the working yarn in front of the stitches, insert the right needle through both stitches from back to front, move the working yarn under the right needle, and pull it with the needle through the stitches, then slip the received stitch from the right needle to the left one* repeat from * to * until the end of the row.

Row 10 (Front Side): Cast on **the same number of stitches** from the chain of bound off stitches as follows: *with the working yarn behind your work, insert the right needle through the front leg of each stitch, from front to back, move the working yarn onto the needle and pull it through the stitch* repeat from * to * until the end of the row.

Row 11 (Back Side): Purl all the stitches.

Repeat rows: 3-11.

Note: At the end of your work, **after the last row 8, work as follows:** purl 1 extra row—**row 9**—for symmetry with rows 1-2, then bind off all the stitches knitwise the last time as follows: *knit 2 together through the back legs, then slip the received stitch from the right needle to the left one* repeat from * to * until the end of the row.

Pattern 2

Cast on a multiple of 6, plus 1 for symmetry and 2 edge stitches. Six-stitch repeat. Repeat rows: 1-2. The edge stitches are not included in the description below and must be added. Slip the first edge stitch, purl the last one as if to purl in knitting through the back leg.

Knit through the back leg, purl as follows: with the working yarn in front of the stitch, insert the right needle through the stitch from back to front, move the working yarn under the right needle, and pull it with

the needle through the stitch. **Note:** The purl stitch that is worked this way sets up the knit stitch to be knitted through the back leg.

Purl as if to purl in knitting through the front leg as follows: with the working yarn in front of the stitch, insert the right needle through the stitch from back to front, wrap the working yarn forward (i.e., from yourself) around the tip of the right needle, then pull it with the right needle through the stitch. **Note:** The purl stitch that is worked this way sets up the knit stitch to be knitted through the front leg.

Description:

Row 1: *Purl 1 as if to purl in knitting through the back leg, knit 5 out of 5 as follows: knit 5 together through the back legs—do not release the left needle yet—yarn over forward (i.e., from yourself), knit these 5 together through the back legs again, yarn over forward (i.e., from yourself), then knit these 5 together through the back legs 1 more time* repeat from * to * until the end of the row before the edge stitch, purl 1 as if to purl in knitting through the back leg.

Row 2: *Knit 1 through the back leg, purl 5 out of 5 as follows: purl 5 together as if to purl in knitting through the front leg, yarn over forward (i.e., from yourself), purl these 5 together as if to purl in knitting through the front leg again, yarn over forward (i.e., from yourself), purl these 5 together as if to purl in knitting through the front leg 1 more time* repeat from * to * until the end of the row before the edge stitch, knit 1 through the back leg.

Repeat rows: 1-2.

Bind off as follows: After the last row 2, turn your work over. The Front Side: slip all the stitches from the left needle to the right one; thus, the working yarn is at the end of the row, then turn your work over. The Back Side: slip 2 stitches purlwise from the left needle to the right one, insert the left needle through the front leg of the 1st slipped stitch from left to right, and pass it over the 2nd stitch (now there is 1 stitch on the right needle) *slip 1 stitch purlwise from the left needle to the right one, insert the left needle through the front leg of the 1st stitch on the right needle from left to right and pass it over the 2nd stitch, now there is 1 stitch on the right needle* repeat from * to * until the end of the row.

Note: For trimming, bind off using larger needles than the working ones to create a larger chain of edge stitches, as this method of binding off creates a tight chain of edge stitches.

Pattern 3

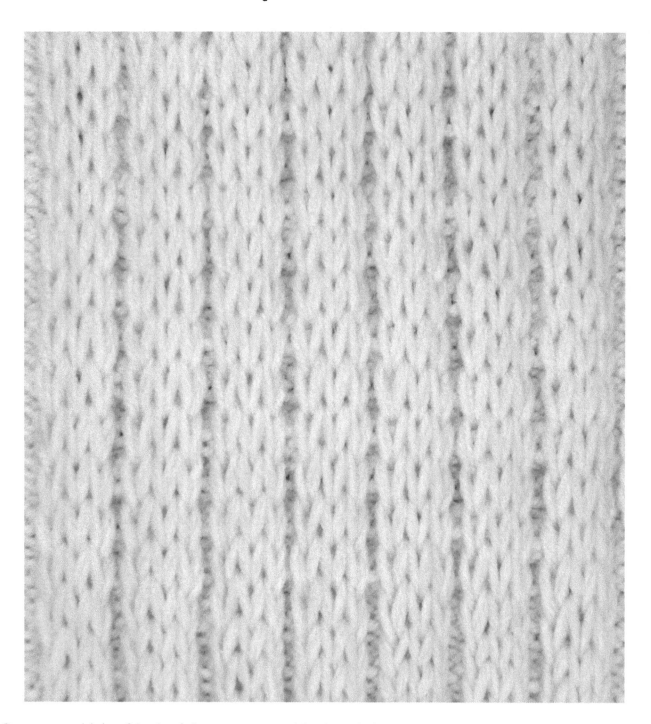

Cast on a multiple of 5, plus 2 for symmetry and 2 edge stitches.

Five-stitch repeat. Repeat rows 1-4. The edge stitches are not included in the description below and must be added. Slip the first edge stitch, purl the last one.

Knit through the back leg, purl as follows: with the working yarn in front of the stitch, insert the right needle through the stitch from back to front, move the working yarn under the right needle, and pull it with

the needle through the stitch. **Note:** The purl stitch that is worked this way sets up the knit stitch to be knitted through the back leg. **Needles: U.S. no.6 (4 mm). Knit tightly. Use a bulky yarn.**

Description:

Row 1: *Purl 2, knit 3 as follows: insert the right needle through the stitch from left to right and wrap the working yarn forward (i.e., from yourself) around the tip of the right needle 2 times, then finish the stitch, as usual,* repeat from * to * until the end of the row before the edge stitch, purl 2.

Row 2: *Knit 2, with the working yarn in front of your work, slip the next 3 purlwise, inserting the right needle from right to left and simultaneously unrolling 3 loops into 3 elongated stitches* repeat from * to * until the end of the row before the edge stitch, knit 2.

Row 3: *Purl 2, with the working yarn behind your work, slip the next 3 purlwise* repeat from * to * until the end of the row before the edge stitch, purl 2.

Row 4: *Knit 2, with the working yarn in front of your work, slip the next 3 purlwise* repeat from * to * until the end of the row before the edge stitch, knit 2.

Repeat rows: 1-4.

Bind off as follows: After the last row 4, turn your work over. The Front Side: slip all the stitches from the left needle to the right one; thus, the working yarn is at the end of the row, then turn your work over. The Back Side: slip 2 stitches purlwise from the left needle to the right one, insert the left needle through the front leg of the 1st slipped stitch from left to right, and pass it over the 2nd stitch (now there is 1 stitch on the right needle) *slip 1 stitch purlwise from the left needle to the right one, insert the left needle through the front leg of the 1st stitch on the right needle from left to right and pass it over the 2nd stitch, now there is 1 stitch on the right needle* repeat from * to * until the end of the row.

Note: For trimming, bind off using larger needles than the working ones to create a larger chain of edge stitches, as this method of binding off creates a tight chain of edge stitches.

Pattern 4

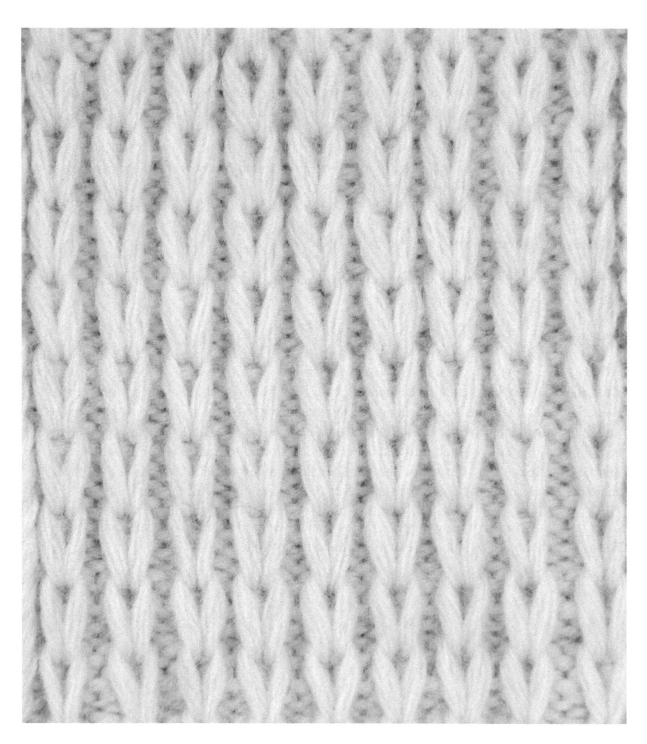

Cast on a multiple of 3, plus 2 for symmetry and 2 edge stitches. Three-stitch repeat. Repeat rows: 1-4. The edge stitches are not included in the description below and must be added. **Slip the first edge stitch; purl the last edge stitch.**

8

Knit through the back leg, purl as follows: with the working yarn in front of the stitch, insert the right needle through the stitch from back to front, move the working yarn under the right needle, and pull it with the needle through the stitch. **Note:** The purl stitch that is worked this way sets up the knit stitch to be knitted through the back leg. **Needles: U.S. no.6 (4 mm). Knit tightly. Use a bulky yarn**.

Description:

Row 1: *Purl 2, knit 1 as follows: insert the right needle through the stitch from left to right and wrap the working yarn forward (i.e., from yourself) around the tip of the right needle 2 times, then finish the knit stitch, as usual,* repeat from * to * until the end of the row before the edge stitch, purl 2.

Row 2: *Knit 2, with the working yarn in front of your work, slip 1 purlwise, simultaneously unrolling the loops into 1 elongated stitch* repeat from * to * until the end of the row before the edge stitch, knit 2.

Row 3: *Purl 2, with the working yarn behind your work slip 1 stitch purlwise* repeat from * to * until the end of the row before the edge stitch, purl 2.

Row 4: *Knit 2, with the working yarn in front of your work slip 1 purlwise* repeat from * to * until the end of the row before the edge stitch, knit 2.

Repeat rows: 1-4.

Bind off as follows: After the last row 4, turn your work over. The Front Side: slip all the stitches from the left needle to the right one; thus, the working yarn is at the end of the row, then turn your work over. The Back Side: slip 2 stitches purlwise from the left needle to the right one, insert the left needle through the front leg of the 1st slipped stitch from left to right, and pass it over the 2nd stitch (now there is 1 stitch on the right needle) *slip 1 stitch purlwise from the left needle to the right one, insert the left needle through the front leg of the 1st stitch on the right needle from left to right and pass it over the 2nd stitch, now there is 1 stitch on the right needle* repeat from * to * until the end of the row.

Note: For trimming, bind off using larger needles than the working ones to create a larger chain of edge stitches, as this method of binding off creates a tight chain of edge stitches.

Pattern 5

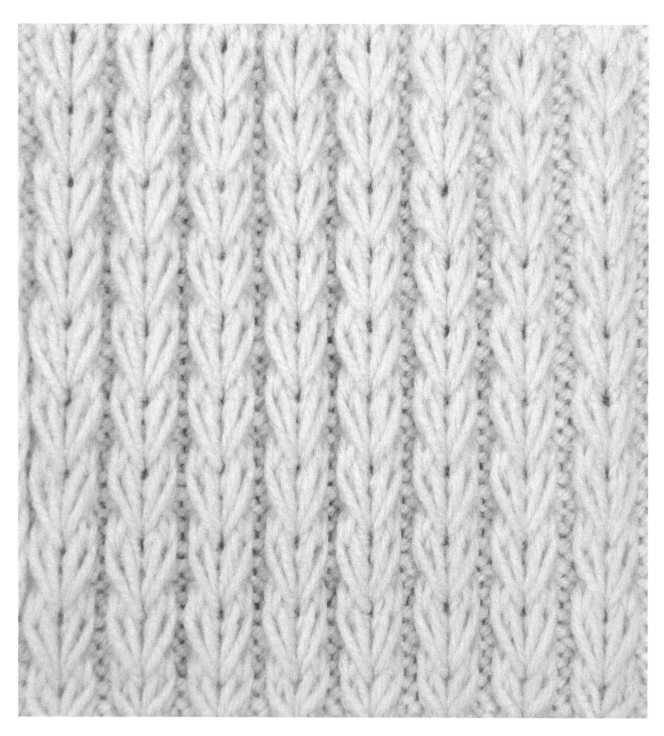

Cast on a multiple of 5, plus 2 for symmetry and 2 edge stitches. Five-stitch repeat. Set up rows: 1-5. Repeat rows: 6-9. The edge stitches are not included in the description below and must be added. Slip the first edge stitch, purl the last one as if to purl in knitting through the back legs as follows: with the working yarn in front of the stitch, insert the right needle through the stitch from back to front, then more the working yarn under the right needle and pull it with the needle through the stitch.

Knit through the front leg, purl as follows: with the working yarn in front of the stitch, insert the right needle through the stitch from back to front, wrap the working yarn forward (i.e., from yourself) around the tip of the right needle, then pull it with the right needle through the stitch. **Note:** The purl stitch that is worked this way sets up the knit stitch to be knitted through the front leg.

Knit tightly. Knit all stitches the same length; the elongated stitches become longer due to slipping them in the cross row.

Description:

Row 1 (set up row): *Knit 2, purl 3* repeat from * to * until the end of the row before the edge stitch, knit 2.

Row 2 (set up row): *purl 2, the next 3 stitches become 5 after knitting them as follows: with the working yarn behind your work, insert the right needle—on the Front Side (FS)—through the center stitch 1 row below and pull the working yarn through this stitch onto the FS, leave the new stitch on the right needle, knit the next 3, then insert the right needle, on the FS, through the same center stitch 1 row below 1 more time and pull the working yarn onto the FS again (this new stitch must have the same length as the 1st new stitch), now there are 5 stitches, instead of the former 3* repeat from * to * until the end of the row before the edge stitch, purl 2.

Row 3 (set up row): *Knit 2, with the working yarn in front of your work, slip 1 purlwise, purl 3, with the working yarn in front of your work slip 1 purlwise* repeat from * to * until the end of the row before the edge stitch, knit 2.

Row 4 (set up row): *Purl 2, swap the next 2 and knit them together as follows: insert the right needle through the 2nd stitch behind the 1st stitch and slip it purlwise onto the right needle; as a result, the 1st stitch is also slipped off the left needle, pick up the 1st stitch back onto the left needle—straight, do not twist the stitch, return the 2nd stitch from the right needle to the left one, inserting the left needle from left to right; thus, these 2 stitches are swapped, now knit them together through the front legs, then knit 1, knit the next 2 together* repeat from * to * until the end of the row before the edge stitch, purl 2.

Row 5 (set up row): *Knit 2, purl 3* repeat from * to * until the end of the row before the edge stitch, knit 2.

Row 6: *Purl 2, the next 3 become 5 after knitting them as follows: with the working yarn behind your work, insert the right needle—on the FS—through the center stitch 4 rows below, count from the center stitch that is on the left needle, and pull the working yarn through this center stitch onto the FS, thus, making 1 new stitch, leave it on the right needle, knit the next 3, then insert the right needle—on the FS—through the same center stitch 4 rows below 1 more time and pull the working yarn through this stitch onto the FS, thus, making the 2nd new stitch, leave the new stitch on the right needle (the 2nd new stitch must have the same length as the 1st stitch), now there are 5 stitches, instead of the former 3* repeat from * to * until the end of the row before the edge stitch, purl 2.

Row 7: *Knit 2, with the working yarn in front of your work slip 1 purlwise, purl 3, with the working yarn in front of your work slip 1 purlwise* repeat from * to * until the end of the row before the edge stitch, knit 2.

Row 8: *Purl 2, slip the next 2 knitwise, swap and replace them on the left needle, then knit them together through the front legs, then knit 1, knit the next 2 together* repeat from * to * until the end of the row before the edge stitch, purl 2.

Row 9: *Knit 2, purl 3* repeat from * to * until the end of the row before the edge stitch, knit 2.

Repeat rows: 6-9.

Bind off as follows: After the last row 9, turn your work over. The Front Side: slip all the stitches from the left needle to the right one; thus, the working yarn is at the end of the row, then turn your work over. The Back Side: slip 2 purlwise from the left needle to the right one, insert the left needle through the front leg of the 1st slipped stitch from left to right, and pass it over the 2nd stitch (now there is 1 stitch on the right needle) *slip 1 purlwise from the left needle to the right one, insert the left needle through the front leg of the 1st stitch on the right needle from left to right and pass it over the 2nd stitch, now there is 1 stitch on the right needle* repeat from * to * until the end of the row.

Note: For trimming, bind off using larger needles than the working ones to create a larger chain of edge stitches, as this method of binding off creates a tight chain of edge stitches.

Pattern 6

Cast on a multiple of 11, plus 2 for symmetry and 2 edge stitches. Eleven-stitch repeat. Repeat rows: 1-10. The edge stitches are not included in the description below and must be added. Slip the first edge stitch; purl the last edge stitch as if to purl in knitting through the back leg as follows: insert the right needle through the stitch from back to front, move the working yarn under the right needle and pull it with the needle through the stitch. **Knit tightly.**

Knit through the front legs; purl as follows: with the working yarn in front of the stitch, insert the right needle through the stitch from back to front, wrap the working yarn forward (i.e., from yourself) around the tip of the right needle, then pull the working yarn with the right needle through the stitch. The purl stitch that is worked this way sets up the knit stitch to be knitted through the front leg.

Description:

Row 1: *Purl 2, knit 1, yarn over forward (i.e., from yourself), knit 1, knit 2 together, purl 1, knit 2 together through the back legs as follows: insert the right needle through the front leg of the 1st stitch from front to back and slip it onto the right needle, insert the right needle through the front leg of the 2nd stitch from front to back and slip it onto the right needle, then return both stitches purlwise onto the left needle, now knit 2 together through the back legs, then knit 1, yarn over forward (i.e., from yourself), knit 1* repeat from * to * until the end of the row before the edge stitch, purl 2.

Row 2: *Knit 2, purl 4, knit 1, purl 4* repeat from * to * until the end of the row before the edge stitch, knit 2.

Row 3: *Purl 2, knit 1, yarn over forward (i.e., from yourself), knit 1, knit 2 together, purl 1, knit 2 together through the back legs as described in row 1, knit 1, yarn over forward (i.e., from yourself), knit 1* repeat from * to * until the end of the row before the edge stitch, purl 2.

Row 4: *Knit 2, purl 4, knit 1, purl 4* repeat from * to * until the end of the row before the edge stitch, knit 2.

Row 5: *Purl 2, knit 2, knit 2 together, yarn over forward (i.e., from yourself), purl 1, yarn over forward (i.e., from yourself), knit 2 together through the back legs as described in row 1, knit 2* repeat from * to * until the end of the row before the edge stitch, purl 2.

Row 6: *Knit 2, purl 4, knit 1, purl 4* repeat from * to * until the end of the row before the edge stitch, knit 2.

Row 7: *Purl 2, knit 1, knit 2 together, yarn over forward (i.e., from yourself), knit 1, purl 1, knit 1, yarn over forward (i.e., from yourself), knit 2 together through the back legs as described in row 1, knit 1* repeat from * to * until the end of the row before the edge stitch, purl 2.

Row 8: *Knit 2, purl 4, knit 1, purl 4* repeat from * to * until the end of the row before the edge stitch, knit 2.

Row 9: *Purl 2, knit 2 together, yarn over forward (i.e., from yourself), knit 2, purl 1, knit 2, yarn over forward (i.e., from yourself), knit 2 together through the back legs as described in row 1* repeat from * to * until the end of the row before the edge stitch, purl 2.

Row 10: *Knit 2, purl 4, knit 1, purl 4* repeat from * to * until the end of the row before the edge stitch, knit 2.

Repeat rows: 1-10.

Bind off as follows: slip the edge stitch onto the right needle, knit the next 1 through the front leg, then insert the left needle through the slipped edge stitch from left to right and pass it over the knitted stitch; *now there is 1 stitch on the right needle; knit the next 1 through the front leg (now there are 2 stitches on the right needle), insert the left needle through the 1st stitch on the right needle from left to right and pass it over the 2nd stitch* repeat from * to * until the end of the row.

Pattern 7

Reversible

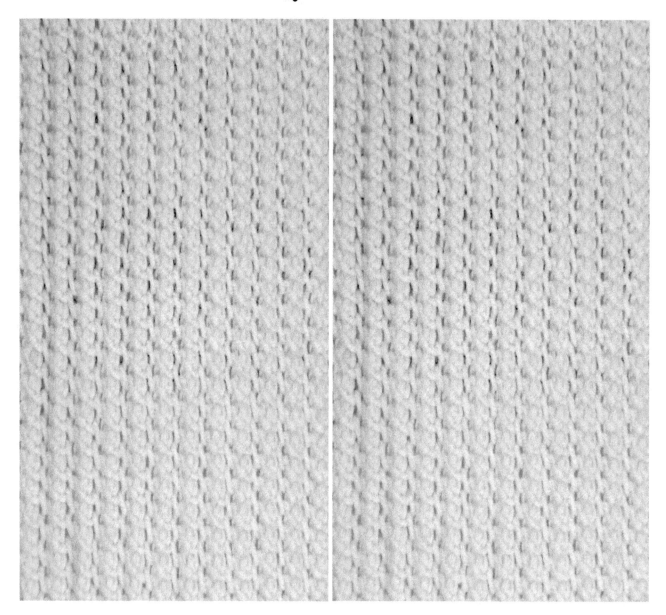

The Front Side   **The Back Side**

Cast on a multiple of 4, plus 2 edge stitches. Four-stitch repeat. Repeat row 1. The edge stitches are not included in the description below and must be added. **Knit the first edge stitch; knit the last edge stitch.**

Description:

Row 1: *Knit 1 through the front leg, with the working yarn behind your work slip the next 1 purlwise, knit the next 2 together through the back legs, yarn over forward (i.e., from yourself)* repeat from * to * until the next of the row.

Repeat row 1.

Bind off as follows: after the last row, turn your work over. Slip all the stitches from the left needle to the right one; thus, the working yarn is at the end of the right needle, then turn your work over. Slip 2 purlwise from the left needle to the right one, insert the left needle through the front leg of the 1st slipped stitch from left to right, and pass it over the 2nd stitch (now there is 1 stitch on the right needle) *slip 1 purlwise from the left needle to the right one, insert the left needle through the front leg of the 1st stitch on the right needle from left to right and pass it over the 2nd stitch, now there is 1 stitch on the right needle* repeat from * to * until the end of the row.

Note: For trimming, bind off using larger needles than the working ones, as this method of binding off stitches creates a tight chain of edge stitches.

Pattern 8

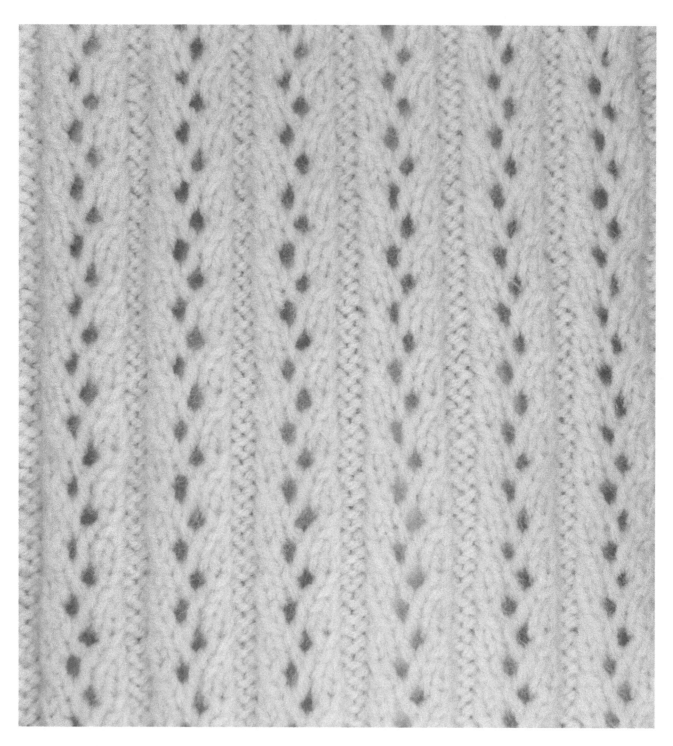

Cast on a multiple of 6, plus 2 for symmetry and 2 edge stitches. Six-stitch repeat. Repeat rows: 1-4. The edge stitches are not included in the description below and must be added. Slip the first edge stitch, purl the last one.

Needles: 2.5 mm.

Knit through the back leg, purl as follows: with the working yarn in front of the stitch, insert the right needle through the stitch from back to front, move the working yarn under the right needle, and pull it with the needle through the stitch. **Note:** The purl stitch that is worked this way sets up the knit stitch to be knitted through the back leg.

Description:

Row 1: *Purl 2, knit 2 together through the front legs as follows: slip the 1st stitch purlwise onto the right needle, insert the right needle through the 2nd stitch from back to front and slip it onto the right needle, thus moving the back leg to the front, return both stitches onto the left needle, now knit 2 together through the front legs, then yarn over forward (i.e., from yourself), knit 2* repeat from * to * until the end of the row before the edge stitch, purl 2.

Row 2: *Knit 2, purl 4* repeat from * to * until the end of the row before the edge stitch, knit 2.

Row 3: *Purl 2, knit 2, yarn over forward (i.e., from yourself), knit 2 together through the back legs as follows: slip the 1st stitch purlwise onto the right needle, insert the right needle through the 2nd stitch from back to front and slip it onto the right needle, thus moving the back leg to the front, return both stitches onto the left needle, now knit 2 together through the back legs* repeat from * to * until the end of the row before the edge stitch, purl 2.

Row 4: *Knit 2, purl 4* repeat from * to * until the end of the row before the edge stitch, knit 2.

Repeat rows: 1-4.

Bind off in ribbing as follows: Slip the edge stitch onto the right needle, purl the next 1, insert the left needle through the 1st stitch on the right needle from left to right, and pass it over the 2nd one (now there is 1 stitch on the right needle), purl the next 1, insert the left needle through the 1st stitch on the right needle from left to right and pass it over the 2nd one (now there is 1 stitch on the right needle), *knit 1, insert the left needle through the 1st stitch on the right needle from left to right and pass it over the 2nd one (now there is 1 stitch on the right needle), bind off the next 3 (knit stitches) the same as the 1st one, then purl 1, insert the left needle through the 1st stitch on the right needle from left to right and pass it over the 2nd one (now there is 1 stitch on the right needle), bind off the next purl stitch the same as the previous one* repeat from * to * until the end of the row; purl the edge stitch, insert the left needle through the 1st stitch on the right needle from left to right and pass it over the 2nd one.

Pattern 9

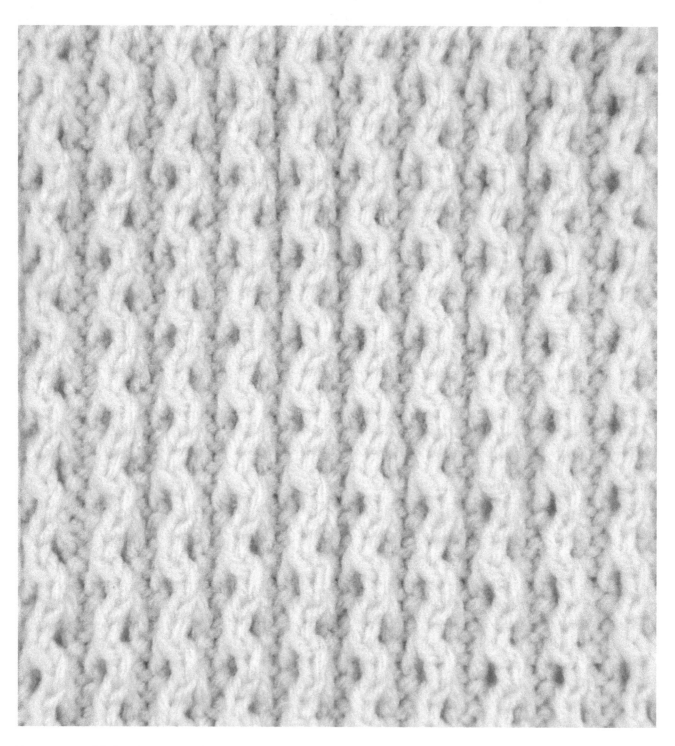

Cast on a multiple of 4, plus 2 for symmetry and 2 edge stitches. Four-stitch repeat. Repeat rows: 1-4. The edge stitches are not included in the description below and must be added. Slip the first edge stitch, purl the last one.

Knit through the back leg, purl as follows: with the working yarn in front of the stitch, insert the right needle through the stitch from back to front, move the working yarn under the right needle, and pull it with the needle through the stitch. **Note:** The purl stitch that is worked this way sets up the knit stitch to be knitted through the back leg. **Knit tightly.**

Description:

Row 1: *Purl 2, yarn over forward (i.e., from yourself), knit 2 together* repeat from * to * until the end of the row before the edge stitch, purl 2.

Row 2: *Knit 2, purl 2* repeat from * to * until the end of the row before the edge stitch, knit 2.

Row 3: *Purl 2, knit 2 together as follows: slip 2 onto the right needle, inserting the right needle from back to front, thus turning these 2 stitches, moving the back legs to the front, then return both stitches onto the left needle and knit them together through the front legs, yarn over forward (i.e., from yourself)* repeat from * to * until the end of the row before the edge stitch, purl 2.

Row 4: *Knit 2, purl 2* repeat from * to * until the end of the row before the edge stitch, knit 2.

Repeat rows: 1-4.

Bind off as follows: After the last row 4, turn your work over. The Front Side: slip all the stitches from the left needle to the right one; thus, the working yarn is at the end of the row; turn your work over. The Back Side: slip 2 purlwise from the left needle to the right one, insert the left needle through the front leg of the 1ˢᵗ slipped stitch from left to right, and pass it over the 2ⁿᵈ stitch (now there is 1 stitch on the right needle) *slip 1 purlwise from the left needle to the right one, insert the left needle through the front leg of the 1ˢᵗ stitch on the right needle from left to right and pass it over the 2ⁿᵈ stitch, now there is 1 stitch on the right needle* repeat from * to * until the end of the row.

Note: For trimming, bind off using larger needles than the working ones to create a larger chain of edge stitches, as this method of binding off creates a tight chain of edge stitches.

Pattern 10

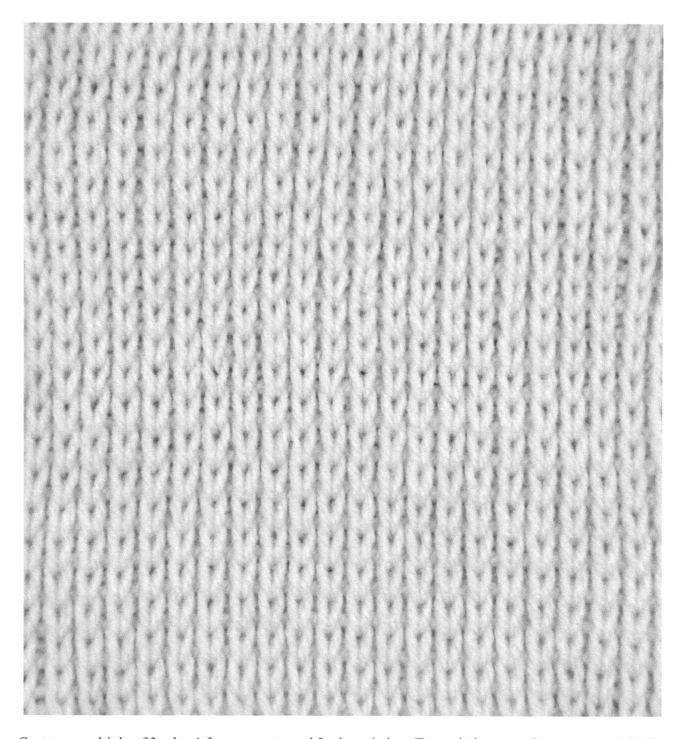

Cast on a multiple of 2, plus 1 for symmetry and 2 edge stitches. Two-stitch repeat. Repeat rows: 1-2. The edge stitches are not included in the description below and must be added. Slip the first edge stitch, purl the last one.

Knit through the back leg, purl as follows: with the working yarn in front of the stitch, insert the right needle through the stitch from back to front, move the working yarn under the right needle, and pull it with the needle through the stitch. **Note:** The purl stitch that is worked this way sets up the knit stitch to be knitted through the back leg. **Knit tightly.**

Description:

Row 1: *Purl 1, with the working yarn behind your work slip 1 purlwise* repeat from * to * until the end of the row before the edge stitch, purl 1.

Row 2: *Knit 1, purl 1 through the back leg* repeat from * to * until the end of the row before the edge stitch, knit 1.

Repeat rows: 1-2.

Bind off as follows: After the last row 2, turn your work over. The Front Side: slip all the stitches from the left needle to the right one; thus, the working yarn is at the end of the row; turn your work over. The Back Side: slip 2 purlwise from the left needle to the right one, insert the left needle through the front leg of the 1st slipped stitch from left to right, and pass it over the 2nd stitch (now there is 1 stitch on the right needle) *slip 1 purlwise from the left needle to the right one, insert the left needle through the front leg of the 1st stitch on the right needle from left to right and pass it over the 2nd stitch, now there is 1 stitch on the right needle* repeat from * to * until the end of the row.

Note: For trimming, bind off using larger needles than the working ones to create a larger chain of edge stitches, as this method of binding off creates a tight chain of edge stitches.

Pattern 11

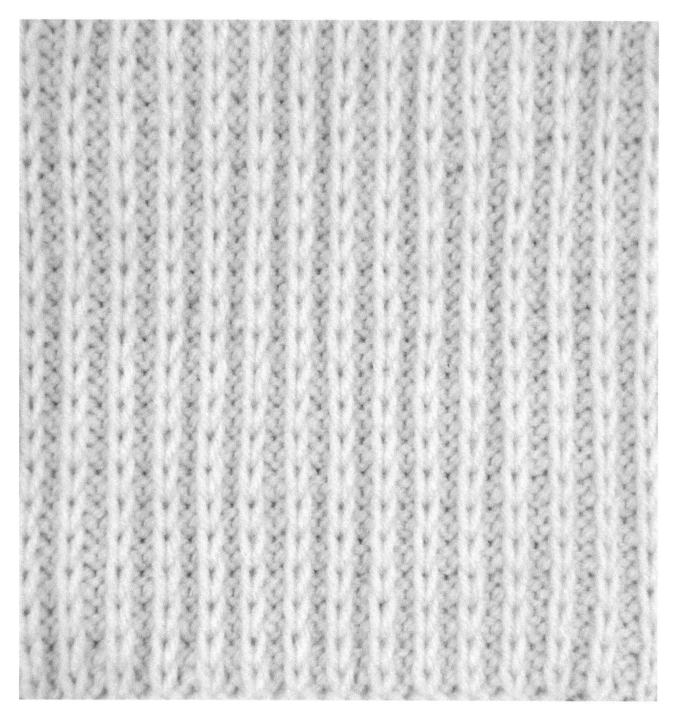

Cast on a multiple of 3, plus 2 for symmetry and 2 edge stitches. Three-stitch repeat. Repeat rows: 1-2. The edge stitches are not included in the description and must be added. Slip the first edge stitch, purl the last one.

Knit through the back leg, purl as follows: with the working yarn in front of the stitch, insert the right needle through the stitch from back to front, move the working yarn under the right needle, and pull it with

the needle through the stitch. **Note:** The purl stitch that is worked this way sets up the knit stitch to be knitted through the back leg. **Knit tightly.**

Description:

Row 1: *Purl 2, with the working yarn behind your work slip 1 purlwise* repeat from * to * until the end of the row before the edge stitch, purl 2.

Row 2: *Knit 2, purl 1 through the back leg* repeat from * to * until the end of the row before the edge stitch, knit 2.

Repeat rows: 1-2.

Bind off as follows: After the last row 2, turn your work over. The Front Side: slip all the stitches from the left needle to the right one; thus, the working yarn is at the end of the row; turn your work over. The Back Side: slip 2 purlwise from the left needle to the right one, insert the left needle through the front leg of the 1st slipped stitch from left to right, and pass it over the 2nd stitch (now there is 1 stitch on the right needle) *slip 1 purlwise from the left needle to the right one, insert the left needle through the front leg of the 1st stitch on the right needle from left to right and pass it over the 2nd stitch, now there is 1 stitch on the right needle* repeat from * to * until the end of the row.

Note: For trimming, bind off using larger needles than the working ones to create a larger chain of edge stitches, as this method of binding off creates a tight chain of edge stitches.

Pattern 12

Cast on a multiple of 3, plus 2 edge stitches. Three-stitch repeat. Repeat rows: 2-5.

The edge stitches are not included in the description below and must be added. Slip the first edge stitch, purl the last one.

Knit through the back leg, purl as follows: with the working yarn in front of the stitch, insert the right needle through the stitch from back to front, move the working yarn under the right needle, and pull it with the needle through the stitch. **Note:** The purl stitch that is worked this way sets up the knit stitch to be knitted through the back leg.

Description:

Row 1: Purl 1 as if to purl in knitting through the back leg, *yarn over forward (i.e., from yourself), with the working yarn behind your work, slip 1 purlwise, purl 2* repeat from * to * until the end of the row before the edge stitch, yarn over forward (i.e., from yourself), with the working yarn behind your work slip 1 purlwise, purl 1 as if to purl in knitting through the back leg.

Row 2: Knit 1 through the back leg, *yarn over forward (i.e., from yourself), with the working yarn behind your work, slip 2 purlwise, knit 2* repeat from * to * until the end of the row before the edge stitch, yarn over forward (i.e., from yourself), with the working yarn behind your work, slip 2 purlwise, knit 1 through the back leg.

Row 3: Purl 1, *yarn over forward (i.e., from yourself), with the working yarn behind your work, slip 3 purlwise, purl 2* repeat from * to * until the end of the row before the edge stitch, yarn over forward (i.e., from yourself), with the working yarn behind your work slip 3 purlwise, purl 1.

Row 4: Yarn over forward (i.e., from yourself, slip 1, inserting the right needle from back to front, knit 4 together through the front legs, *yarn over forward (i.e., from yourself), slip 1 purlwise, inserting the right needle from back to front, yarn over forward (i.e., from yourself) 1 more time, slip 1, inserting the right needle from back to front, knit 4 together through the front legs* repeat from * to * before the edge stitch, yarn over forward (i.e., from yourself), slip 1, inserting the right needle from back to front.

Row 5: *Purl 2 together as if to purl in knitting through the back legs, yarn over forward (i.e., from yourself), with the working yarn behind your work slip 1 purlwise, purl 2 together as if to purl in knitting through the back legs* repeat from * to * until the end of the row.

Repeat rows: 2-5.

Bind off as follows: After the last row 5, turn your work over. The Back Side: slip all the stitches from the left needle to the right one; thus, the working yarn is at the end of the row; turn your work over. The Front Side: slip 2 purlwise from the left needle to the right one, insert the left needle through the front leg of the 1st slipped stitch from left to right, and pass it over the 2nd stitch (now there is 1 stitch on the right needle) *slip 1 purlwise from the left needle to the right one, insert the left needle through the front leg of the 1st stitch on the right needle from left to right and pass it over the 2nd stitch, now there is 1 stitch on the right needle* repeat from * to * until the end of the row.

Note: For trimming, bind off using larger needles than the working ones to create a larger chain of edge stitches, as this method of binding off creates a tight chain of edge stitches.

Pattern 13

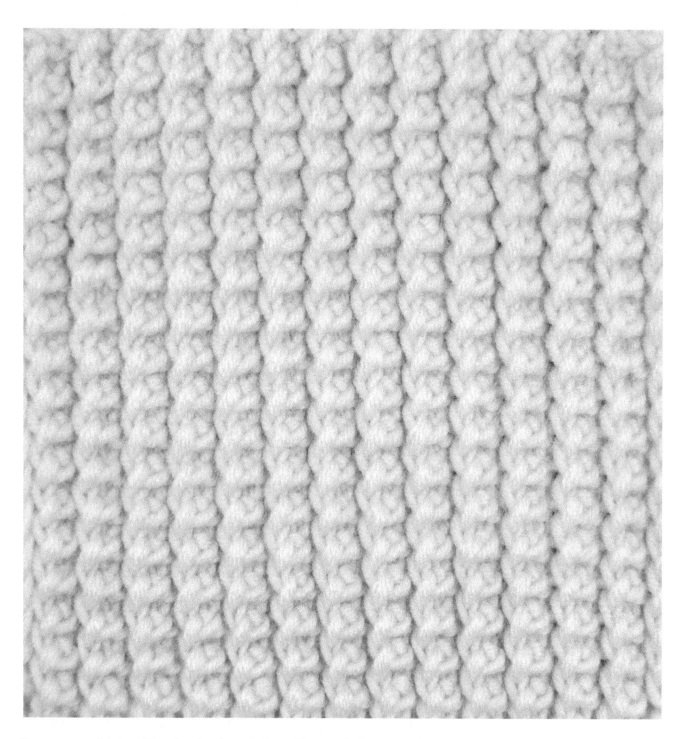

Cast on a multiple of 3, plus 2 edge stitches. Three-stitch repeat. Repeat rows 1-2.

The edge stitches are not included in the description below and must be added. Slip the first edge stitch, purl the last one.

Knit through the back leg, purl as follows: with the working yarn in front of the stitch, insert the right needle through the stitch from back to front, move the working yarn under the right needle, and pull it with the needle through the stitch. **Note:** The purl stitch that is worked this way sets up the knit stitch to be knitted through the back leg. **Use a bulky yarn.**

Description:

Row 1: *Knit 1 through the back leg, yarn over forward (i.e., from yourself), knit 2 through the front legs, then insert the left needle through the yarn over and pass it over these 2 knitted stitches* repeat from * to * until the end of the row.

Row 2: *Knit 2 through the front legs, purl 1 as if to purl in knitting through the back leg* repeat from * to * until the end of the row.

Repeat rows: 1-2.

Bind off as follows: After the last row 2, turn your work over. The Front Side: slip all the stitches from the left needle to the right one; thus, the working yarn is at the end of the row; turn your work over. The Back Side: slip 2 purlwise from the left needle to the right one, insert the left needle through the front leg of the 1st slipped stitch from left to right, and pass it over the 2nd stitch (now there is 1 stitch on the right needle) *slip 1 purlwise from the left needle to the right one, insert the left needle through the front leg of the 1st stitch on the right needle from left to right and pass it over the 2nd stitch, now there is 1 stitch on the right needle* repeat from * to * until the end of the row.

Note: For trimming, bind off using larger needles than the working ones to create a larger chain of edge stitches, as this method of binding off creates a tight chain of edge stitches.

Pattern 14

Reversible

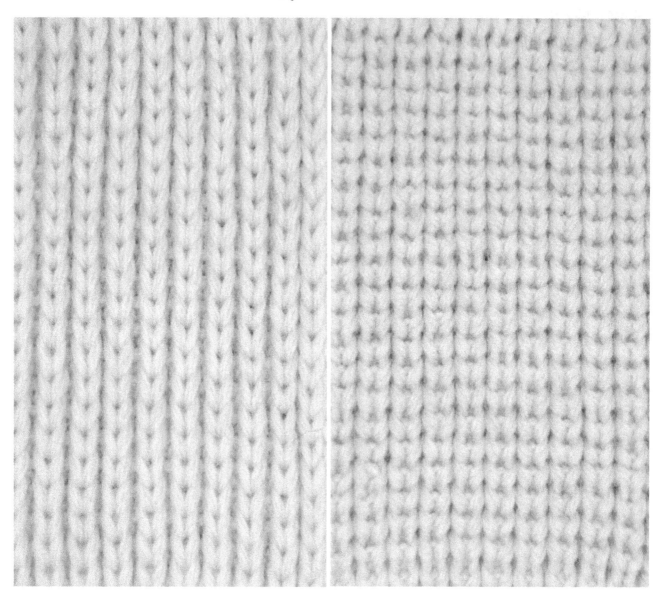

The Front Side   **The Back Side**

Cast on a multiple of 2, plus 2 edge stitches. Two-stitch repeat. Repeat rows: 1-2. The edge stitches are not included in the description below and must be added. Slip the first edge stitch, purl the last one.

Knit through the back leg, purl as follows: with the working yarn in front of the stitch, insert the right needle through the stitch from back to front, move the working yarn under the right needle, and pull it with the needle through the stitch. **Note:** The purl stitch that is worked this way sets up the knit stitch to be knitted through the back leg. **Knit tightly. Use a bulky yarn.**

Description:

Row 1: *Knit 1 stitch through the back leg, with the working yarn in front of your work slip 1 purlwise, yarn over forward (i.e., from yourself)* repeat from * to * until the end of the row.

Row 2: *Knit 1 through the front leg together with yarn over, purl 1 as if to purl in knitting through the back leg* repeat from * to * until the end of the row.

Repeat rows: 1-2.

Bind off as follows: After the last row 2, turn your work over. The Front Side: slip all the stitches from the left needle to the right one; thus, the working yarn is at the end of the row; turn your work over. The Back Side: slip 2 purlwise from the left needle to the right one, insert the left needle through the front leg of the 1st slipped stitch from left to right, and pass it over the 2nd stitch (now there is 1 stitch on the right needle) *slip 1 purlwise from the left needle to the right one, insert the left needle through the front leg of the 1st stitch on the right needle from left to right and pass it over the 2nd stitch, now there is 1 stitch on the right needle* repeat from * to * until the end of the row.

Note: For trimming, bind off using larger needles than the working ones to create a larger chain of edge stitches, as this method of binding off creates a tight chain of edge stitches.

Pattern 15

Reversible

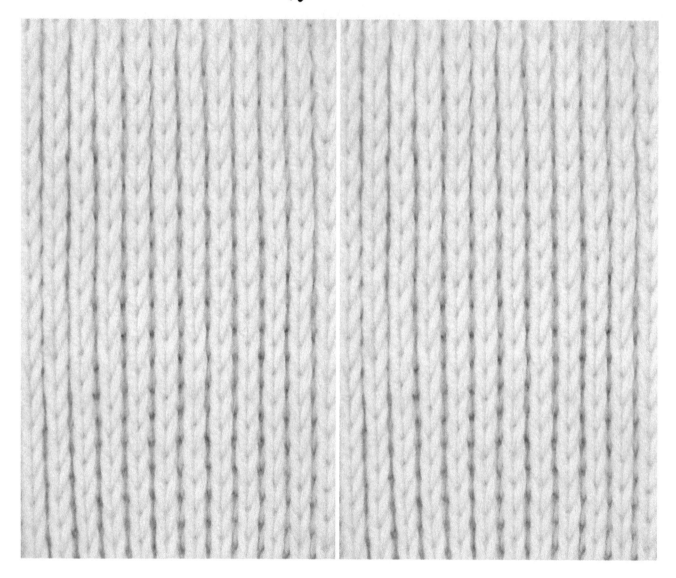

The Front Side   **The Back Side**

Cast on a multiple of 2, plus 2 edge stitches. Two-stitch repeat. Repeat row: 2.

The edge stitches are not included in the description below and must be added. Slip the first edge stitch, purl the last one.

Knit through the back leg, purl as follows: with the working yarn in front of the stitch, insert the right needle through the stitch from back to front, move the working yarn under the right needle, and pull it with the needle through the stitch. The purl stitch that is worked this way sets up the knit stitch to be knitted through the back leg. **Use a bulky yarn.**

Description:

Row 1 (set up row): *Knit 1, purl 1* repeat from * to * until the end of the row.

Row 2: *Knit 1 as follows: insert the right needle through the stitch 1 row below and knit it, as usual, purl the next 1* repeat from * to * until the end of the row.

Repeat row: 2.

Bind off as follows: After the last row 2, turn your work over. The Front Side: slip all the stitches from the left needle to the right one; thus, the working yarn is at the end of the row; turn your work over. The Back Side: slip 2 purlwise from the left needle to the right one, insert the left needle through the front leg of the 1st slipped stitch from left to right, and pass it over the 2nd stitch (now there is 1 stitch on the right needle) *slip 1 purlwise from the left needle to the right one, insert the left needle through the front leg of the 1st stitch on the right needle from left to right and pass it over the 2nd stitch, now there is 1 stitch on the right needle* repeat from * to * until the end of the row.

Note: For trimming, bind off using larger needles than the working ones to create a larger chain of edge stitches, as this method of binding off creates a tight chain of edge stitches.

Pattern 16

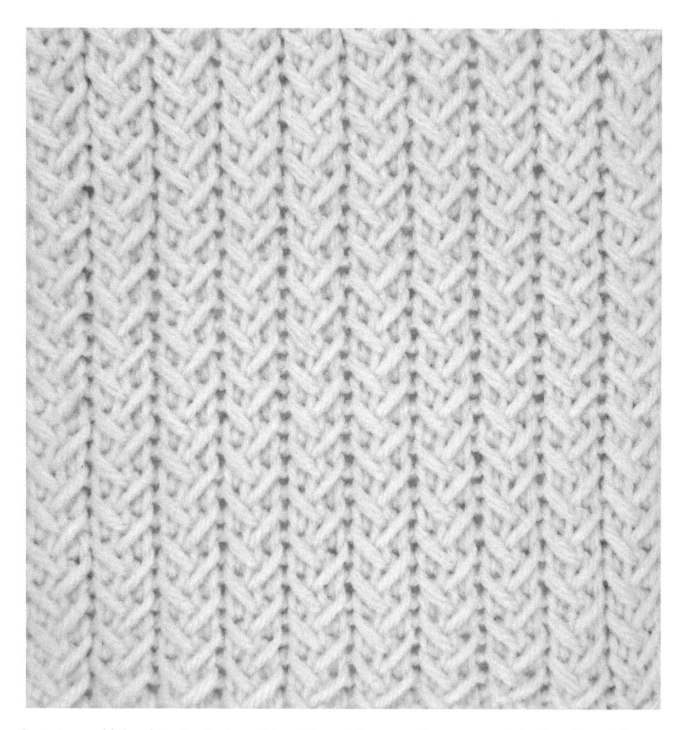

Cast on a multiple of 5, plus 2 edge stitches. Five-stitch repeat. Repeat rows: 1-2. The edge stitches are not included in the description below and must be added. Slip the first edge stitch, purl the last one.

Knit through the back leg, purl as follows: with the working yarn in front of the stitch, insert the right needle through the stitch from back to front, move the working yarn under the right needle, and pull it with

34

the needle through the stitch. The purl stitch that is worked this way sets up the knit stitch to be knitted through the back leg.

Description:

Row 1: *Knit 2, knit 3 together as follows: knit 3 together through the back legs—do not release the left needle yet—make a yarn over forward (i.e., from yourself), knit 1 through the back leg, then slip 2 off the left needle and leave them as they are* repeat from * to * until the end of the row.

Row 2: Purl 2, purl the next 3 together as follows: purl 3 together—do not release the left needle yet—make a yarn over backward (i.e., to yourself), purl 1, then slip the next 2 off the left needle and leave them as they are* repeat from * to * until the end of the row.

Repeat rows: 1-2.

Bind off as follows: After the last row 2, turn your work over. The Front Side: slip all the stitches from the left needle to the right one; thus, the working yarn is at the end of the row; turn your work over. The Back Side: slip 2 purlwise from the left needle to the right one, insert the left needle through the front leg of the 1st slipped stitch from left to right, and pass it over the 2nd stitch (now there is 1 stitch on the right needle) *slip 1 purlwise from the left needle to the right one, insert the left needle through the front leg of the 1st stitch on the right needle from left to right and pass it over the 2nd stitch, now there is 1 stitch on the right needle* repeat from * to * until the end of the row.

Note: For trimming, bind off using larger needles than the working ones to create a larger chain of edge stitches, as this method of binding off creates a tight chain of edge stitches.

Pattern 17

Reversible

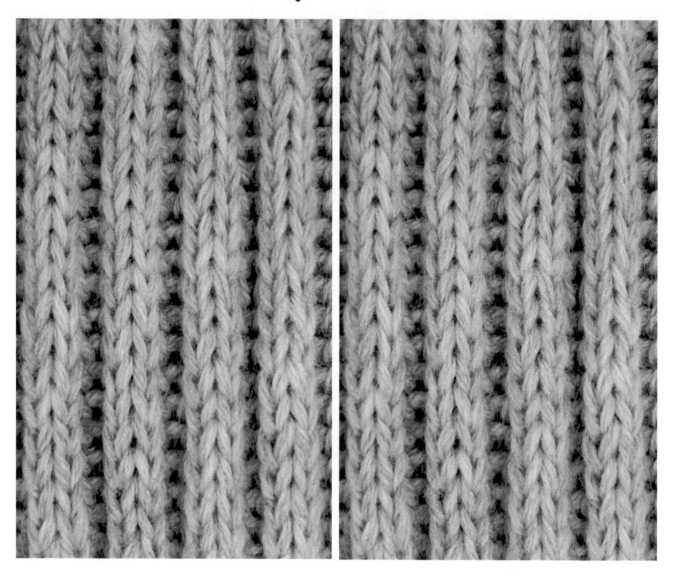

The Front Side   The Back Side

36

Cast on a multiple of 4, plus 2 edge stitches. Four-stitch repeat. Repeat row: 2.

The edge stitches are not included in the description below and must be added. Slip the first edge stitch, purl the last one.

Knit through the back leg, purl as follows: with the working yarn in front of the stitch, insert the right needle through the stitch from back to front, move the working yarn under the right needle, and pull it with the needle through the stitch. **Note:** The purl stitch that is worked this way sets up the knit stitch to be knitted through the back leg. **Knit tightly. Use a bulky yarn.**

Description:

Row 1 (set up row): *Knit 2, purl 2* repeat from * to * until the end of the row.

Row 2: *Knit 2 as follows: insert the right needle through the stitch of the previous row (i.e., 1 row below) and knit it as usual through the back leg, knit the next one the same as the 1st stitch, purl 2* repeat from * to * until the end of the row.

Repeat row: 2.

Bind off as follows: After the last row 2, turn your work over. The Front Side: slip all the stitches from the left needle to the right one; thus, the working yarn is at the end of the row; turn your work over. The Back Side: slip 2 purlwise from the left needle to the right one, insert the left needle through the front leg of the 1st slipped stitch from left to right, and pass it over the 2nd stitch (now there is 1 stitch on the right needle) *slip 1 purlwise from the left needle to the right one, insert the left needle through the front leg of the 1st stitch on the right needle from left to right and pass it over the 2nd stitch, now there is 1 stitch on the right needle* repeat from * to * until the end of the row.

Note: For trimming, bind off using larger needles than the working ones to create a larger chain of edge stitches, as this method of binding off creates a tight chain of edge stitches.

Pattern 18

Reversible

The Front Side   **The Back Side**

Cast on a multiple of 2, plus 2 edge stitches. Two-stitch repeat. Repeat row: 2. The edge stitches are not included in the description below and must be added. Slip the first edge stitch, purl the last one. **Note:** Work knit stitches through the front legs; otherwise, the design distorts. **Knit tightly. Use a bulky yarn.**

Description:

Row 1 (set up row): *Knit 1 through the front leg, yarn over forward (i.e., from yourself), with the working yarn in front of your work slip 1 purlwise* repeat from * to * until the end of the row.

Row 2: *Knit 1 together with the yarn over of the previous row through the front legs, yarn over forward (i.e., from yourself), with the working yarn in front of your work slip 1 (purl stitch) purlwise* repeat from * to * until the end of the row.

Repeat row: 2.

Note: Bind off 1 stitch and yarn over as 1 stitch.

Bind off as follows: After the last row, turn your work over. The Back Side: slip all the stitches from the left needle to the right one; thus, the working yarn is at the end of the row; turn your work over. The Front Side: slip 2 purlwise from the left needle to the right one, insert the left needle through the front leg of the 1st slipped stitch from left to right, and pass it over the 2nd stitch (now there is 1 stitch on the right needle) *slip 1 purlwise from the left needle to the right one purlwise, insert the left needle through the front leg of the 1st stitch on the right needle from left to right and pass it over the 2nd stitch, now there is 1 stitch on the right needle* repeat from * to * until the end of the row.

Note: For trimming, bind off using larger needles than the working ones to create a larger chain of edge stitches, as this method of binding off creates a tight chain of edge stitches.

Pattern 19

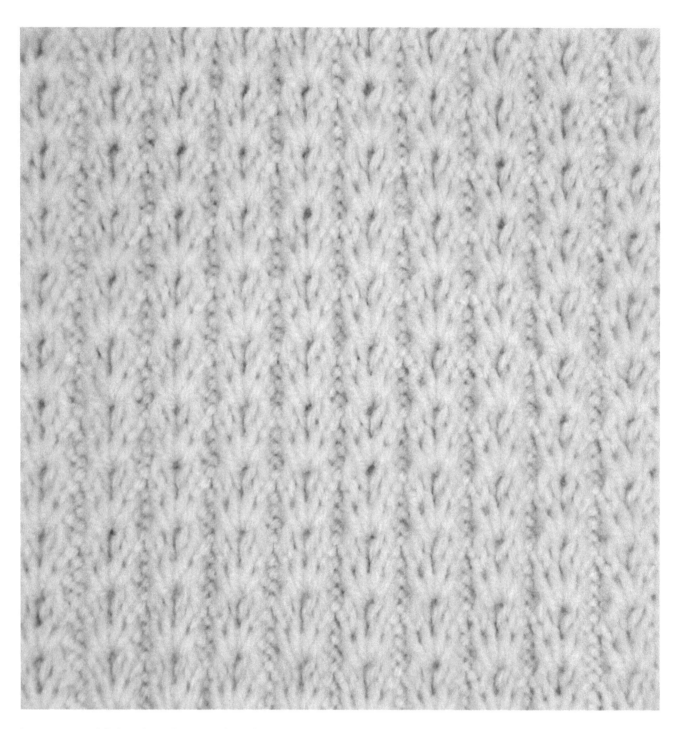

Cast on a multiple of 4, plus 3 and 2 edge stitches. Four-stitch repeat. Repeat rows: 1-4.

The edge stitches are not included in the description below and must be added. Slip the first edge stitch, purl the last one as if to purl in knitting through the back leg.

Knit through the front leg, knit through the back leg, purl as if to purl in knitting through the back leg as follows: with the working yarn in front of the stitch, insert the right needle through the stitch from back to front, move the working yarn under the right needle, and pull it with the needle through the stitch. **Note:** The purl stitch that is worked this way sets up the knit stitch to be knitted through the back leg. **Knit tightly.**

Description:

Row 1: Knit 1 through the front leg, *yarn over forward (i.e., from yourself), slip 1 purlwise, knit 1 through the front leg, knit 1 through the back leg, knit 1 through the front leg* repeat from * to * until the end of the row before the edge stitch, yarn over forward (i.e., from yourself), slip 1 purlwise, knit 1 through the front leg.

Row 2: Purl 1 as if to purl in knitting through the back leg, *yarn over forward (i.e., from yourself), slip 2 purlwise, purl 3 as if to purl in knitting through the back legs* repeat from * to * until the end of the row before the edge stitch, yarn over forward (i.e., from yourself), slip 2 purlwise, then purl 1 as if to purl in knitting through the back leg.

Row 3: Knit 1 through the back leg, *purl 3 together as if to purl in knitting through the back legs twice as follows: purl 3 together—do not release the left needle—yarn over forward (i.e., from yourself), then purl these 3 together 1 more time, then knit 3 through the back legs* repeat from * to * until the end of the row before the edge stitch, purl 3 together as if to purl in knitting through the back legs twice as described at the beginning of the row, then knit 1 through the back leg.

Row 4: *Knit 2 together through the front legs as follows: slip the 1st stitch purlwise onto the right needle, slip the 2nd stitch onto the right needle, inserting the right needle from back to front, thus turning the stitch, then return both stitches onto the left needle and knit them together through the front legs, knit the next 1 through the front leg, knit 2 together through the back legs, purl 1 as if to purl in knitting through the back leg* repeat from * to * until the end of the row before the edge stitch, knit 2 together through the front legs as described at the beginning of the row, knit 1 through the front leg, knit 2 together through the back legs.

Repeat rows: 1-4.

Bind off as follows: After the last row 4, turn your work over. The Front Side: slip all the stitches from the left needle to the right one; thus, the working yarn is at the end of the row; turn your work over. The Back Side: slip 2 purlwise from the left needle to the right one, insert the left needle through the front leg of the 1st slipped stitch from left to right, and pass it over the 2nd stitch (now there is 1 stitch on the right needle) *slip 1 purlwise from the left needle to the right one, insert the left needle through the front leg of the 1st stitch on the right needle from left to right and pass it over the 2nd stitch, now there is 1 stitch on the right needle* repeat from * to * until the end of the row.

Note: For trimming, bind off using larger needles than the working ones to create a larger chain of edge stitches, as this method of binding off creates a tight chain of edge stitches.

Pattern 20

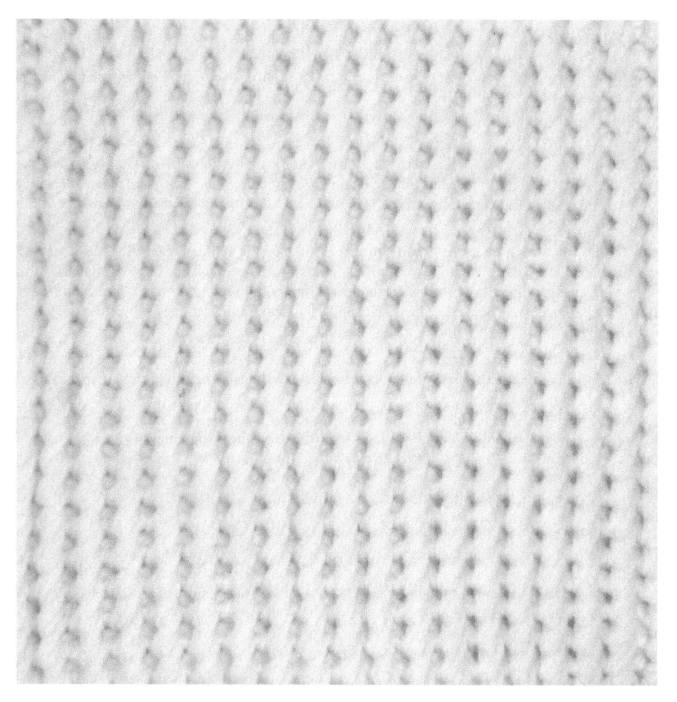

Cast on a multiple of 2, plus 1 for symmetry and 2 edge stitches. Two-stitch repeat. Repeat row: 2-3. The edge stitches are not included in the description below and must be added. Slip the first edge stitch, purl the last one.

Knit through the back leg, purl as follows: with the working yarn in front of the stitch, insert the right needle through the stitch from back to front, move the working yarn under the right needle, and pull it with

the needle through the stitch. **Note:** The purl stitch that is worked this way sets up the knit stitch to be knitted through the back leg.

Description:

Row 1 (set up row, Back Side): *Knit 1, purl 1* repeat from * to * until the end of the row before the edge stitch, knit 1.

Row 2: Purl 1, *with the working yarn behind your work, insert the right needle between the next 2 stitches through space 1 row below and pull the working yarn onto the Front Side (make this stitch the same length as the next stitch), then slip the next stitch purlwise onto the right needle, purl the next 1* repeat from * to * until the end of the row.

Row 3: *Knit 1, purl 2 together* repeat from * to * until the end of the row before the edge stitch, knit 1.

Repeat rows: 2-3.

Bind off as follows: After the last row 3, turn your work over. The Front Side: slip all the stitches from the left needle to the right one; thus, the working yarn is at the end of the row; turn your work over. The Back Side: slip 2 purlwise from the left needle to the right one, insert the left needle through the front leg of the 1st slipped stitch from left to right, and pass it over the 2nd stitch (now there is 1 stitch on the right needle) *slip 1 purlwise from the left needle to the right one, insert the left needle through the front leg of the 1st stitch on the right needle from left to right and pass it over the 2nd stitch, now there is 1 stitch on the right needle* repeat from * to * until the end of the row.

Note: For trimming, bind off using larger needles than the working ones to create a larger chain of edge stitches, as this method of binding off creates a tight chain of edge stitches.

Pattern 21

Cast on a multiple of 3, plus 2 and 2 edge stitches. Three-stitch repeat. Repeat rows: 1-2. The edge stitches are not included in the description below and must be added. Slip the first edge stitch, purl the last one as if to purl in knitting through the back leg as follows: with the working yarn in front of the stitch, insert the right needle through the stitch from back to front, then move the working yarn under the right needle and pull it with the needle through the stitch.

Knit through the front leg, purl as follows: with the working yarn in front of the stitch, insert the right needle through the stitch from back to front, wrap the working yarn forward (i.e., from yourself) around the tip of the right needle, then pull it with the right needle through the stitch. **Note:** The purl stitch that is worked this way sets up the knit stitch to be knitted through the front leg. **Use a bulky yarn.**

Description:

Row 1 (Back Side): *Knit 2, with the working yarn in front of your work slip 1 purlwise, yarn over forward (i.e., from yourself)* repeat from * to * until the end of the row before the edge stitch, knit 2.

Row 2: *Purl 2, knit 2 together* repeat from * to * until the end of the row before the edge stitch, purl 2.

Repeat rows: 1-2.

Bind off as follows: After the last row 2, turn your work over. The Front Side: slip all the stitches from the left needle to the right one; thus, the working yarn is at the end of the row; turn your work over. The Back Side: slip 2 purlwise from the left needle to the right one, insert the left needle through the front leg of the 1st slipped stitch from left to right, and pass it over the 2nd stitch (now there is 1 stitch on the right needle) *slip 1 purlwise from the left needle to the right one, insert the left needle through the front leg of the 1st stitch on the right needle from left to right and pass it over the 2nd stitch, now there is 1 stitch on the right needle* repeat from * to * until the end of the row.

Note: For trimming, bind off using larger needles than the working ones to create a larger chain of edge stitches, as this method of binding off creates a tight chain of edge stitches.

Pattern 22

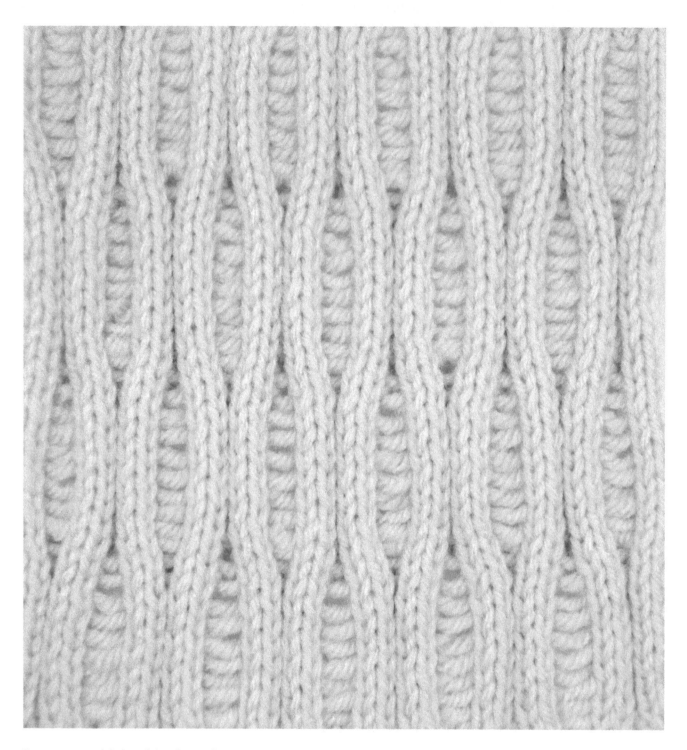

Cast on a multiple of 8, plus 6 for symmetry and 2 edge stitches. Eight-stitch repeat. Repeat rows: 11-30. The edge stitches are not included in the description below and must be added. Slip the first edge stitch, purl the last one.

Knit through the back leg, purl as follows: with the working yarn in front of the stitch, insert the right needle through the stitch from back to front, move the working yarn under the right needle, and pull it with the needle through the stitch. **Note:** The purl stitch that is worked this way sets up the knit stitch to be knitted through the back leg.

Description:

Row 1 (Back Side): Purl 2, *knit 2, purl 2, knit 1, yarn over forward (i.e., from yourself), knit 1, purl 2* repeat from * to * before the edge stitch, knit 2, purl 2.

Row 2: Work the stitches as they are seen: Knit 2, purl 2, *knit 2, purl 3 (**Note:** purl yarn overs of the previous row), knit 2, purl 2* repeat from * to * until the end of the row before the edge stitch, knit 2.

Row 3: Work the stitches as they are seen: Purl 2, *knit 2, purl 2, knit 3, purl 2* repeat from * to * until the end of the row before the edge stitch, knit 2, purl 2.

Row 4: Work the stitches as they are seen: Knit 2, purl 2, *knit 2, purl 3, knit 2, purl 2* repeat from * to * until the end of the row before the edge stitch, knit 2.

Row 5: Work the stitches as they are seen: Purl 2, *knit 2, purl 2, knit 3, purl 2* repeat from * to * until the end of the row before the edge stitch, knit 2, purl 2.

Row 6: Work the stitches as they are seen: Knit 2, purl 2, *knit 2, purl 3, knit 2, purl 2* repeat from * to * until the end of the row before the edge stitch, knit 2.

Row 7: Work the stitches as they are seen: Purl 2, *knit 2, purl 2, knit 3, purl 2* repeat from * to * until the end of the row before the edge stitch, knit 2, purl 2.

Row 8: Work the stitches as they are seen: Knit 2, purl 2, *knit 2, purl 3, knit 2, purl 2* repeat from * to * until the end of the row before the edge stitch, knit 2.

Row 9: Work the stitches as they are seen: Purl 2, *knit 2, purl 2, knit 3, purl 2* repeat from * to * until the end of the row before the edge stitch, knit 2, purl 2.

Row 10: Work the stitches as they are seen: Knit 2, purl 2, *knit 2, purl 3, knit 2, purl 2* repeat from * to * until the end of the row before the edge stitch, knit 2.

Row 11 (Back Side): Purl 2, *knit 1, yarn over forward (i.e., from yourself), knit 1, purl 2, knit 1, slip 1 off the left needle and leave it as is, knit 1, purl 2* repeat from * to * until the end of the row before the edge stitch, knit 1, yarn over forward (i.e., from yourself), knit 1, purl 2.

Note: Slip down the slipped stitches until the row in which the yarn overs were made.

Row 12: Work the stitches as they are seen: Knit 2, purl 3 (**Note:** purl yarn overs of the previous row), *knit 2, purl 2, knit 2, purl 3* repeat from * to * until the end of the row before the edge stitch, knit 2.

Row 13: Work the stitches as they are seen: Purl 2, *knit 3, purl 2, knit 2, purl 2* repeat from * to * until the end of the row before the edge stitch, knit 3, purl 2.

Row 14: Work the stitches as they are seen: Knit 2, purl 3, *knit 2, purl 2, knit 2, purl 3* repeat from * to * until the end of the row before the edge stitch, knit 2.

Row 15: Work the stitches as they are seen: Purl 2, *knit 3, purl 2, knit 2, purl 2* repeat from * to * until the end of the row before the edge stitch, knit 3, purl 2.

Row 16: Work the stitches as they are seen: Knit 2, purl 3, *knit 2, purl 2, knit 2, purl 3* repeat from * to * until the end of the row, before the edge stitch, knit 2.

Row 17: Work the stitches as they are seen: Purl 2, *knit 3, purl 2, knit 2, purl 2* repeat from * to * until the end of the row before the edge stitch, knit 3, purl 2.

Row 18: Work the stitches as they are seen: Knit 2, purl 3, *knit 2, purl 2, knit 2, purl 3* repeat from * to * until the end of the row before the edge stitch, knit 2.

Row 19: Work the stitches as they are seen: Purl 2, *knit 3, purl 2, knit 2, purl 2* repeat from * to * until the end of the row before the edge stitch, knit 3, purl 2.

Row 20: Work the stitches as they are seen: Knit 2, purl 3, *knit 2, purl 2, knit 2, purl 3* repeat from * to * until the end of the row before the edge stitch, knit 2.

Row 21 (Back Side): Purl 2, *knit 1, slip 1 off the left needle and leave it as is, knit 1, purl 2, knit 1, yarn over forward (i.e., from yourself), knit 1, purl 2 * repeat from * to * until the end of the row before the edge stitch, knit 1, slip 1 off the left needle and leave it as is, knit 1, purl 2.

Note: Slip down the slipped stitches until the row in which the yarn overs were made.

Row 22: Work the stitches as they are seen: Knit 2, purl 2, *knit 2, purl 3 (**Note:** purl yarn overs of the previous row), knit 2, purl 2* repeat from * to * until the end of the row before the edge stitch, knit 2.

Row 23: Work the stitches as they are seen: Purl 2, *knit 2, purl 2, knit 3, purl 2* repeat from * to * until the end of the row before the edge stitch, knit 2, purl 2.

Row 24: Work the stitches as they are seen: Knit 2, purl 2, *knit 2, purl 3, knit 2, purl 2* repeat from * to * until the end of the row before the edge stitch, knit 2.

Row 25: Work the stitches as they are seen: Purl 2, *knit 2, purl 2, knit 3, purl 2* repeat from * to * until the end of the row before the edge stitch, knit 2, purl 2.

Row 26: Work the stitches as they are seen: Knit 2, purl 2, *knit 2, purl 3, knit 2, purl 2* repeat from * to * until the end of the row before the edge stitch, knit 2.

Row 27: Work the stitches as they are seen: Purl 2, *Knit 2, purl 2, knit 3, purl 2* repeat from * to * until the end of the row before the edge stitch, knit 2, purl 2.

Row 28: Work the stitches as they are seen: Knit 2, purl 2, *knit 2, purl 3, knit 2, purl 2* repeat from * to * until the end of the row before the edge stitch, knit 2.

Row 29: Work the stitches as they are seen: Purl 2, *knit 2, purl 2, knit 3, purl 2* repeat from * to * until the end of the row before the edge stitch, knit 2, purl 2.

Row 30: Work the stitches as they are seen: Knit 2, purl 2, *knit 2, purl 3, knit 2, purl 2* repeat from * to * until the end of the row before the edge stitch, knit 2.

Repeat rows: 11-30.

Bind off as follows: After the last row 11, turn your work over. The Front Side: slip all the stitches from the left needle to the right one; thus, the working yarn is at the end of the row; turn your work over. The Back Side: slip 2 purlwise from the left needle to the right one, insert the left needle through the front leg of the 1st slipped stitch from left to right, and pass it over the 2nd stitch (now there is 1 stitch on the right needle) *slip 1 purlwise from the left needle to the right one, insert the left needle through the front leg of the 1st stitch on the right needle from left to right and pass it over the 2nd stitch, now there is 1 stitch on the right needle* repeat from * to * until the end of the row.

Note: For trimming, bind off using larger needles than the working ones to create a larger chain of edge stitches, as this method of binding off creates a tight chain of edge stitches.

Pattern 23

Reversible

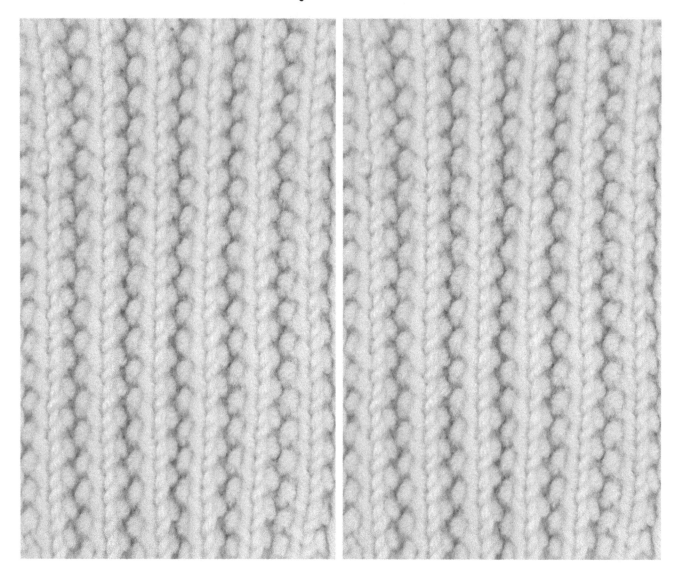

The Front Side   **The Back Side**

Cast on a multiple of 4, plus 1 for symmetry and 2 edge stitches. Two-stitch repeat. Repeat rows: 1-2. The edge stitches are not included in the description below and must be added. Slip the first edge stitch, purl the last one.

Knit through the back leg, purl as follows: with the working yarn in front of the stitch, insert the right needle through the stitch from back to front, move the working yarn under the right needle, and pull it with the needle through the stitch. **Note:** The purl stitch that is worked this way sets up the knit stitch to be knitted through the back leg.

Note: This pattern is loose when it is knitted through the front legs (conventionally) and is tighter when it is knitted through the back legs. If you choose to knit it through the front legs, do not switch the legs of the 2nd stitches in the knit and purl pairs. Knit all stitches as they are seen. **Knit tightly anyway. Use a bulky yarn.**

Description:

Row 1: *Knit 2 through the back legs as follows: before knitting the 2nd stitch, change the legs, moving the front leg to the back, inserting the right needle from the front side, releasing the left needle from the stitch, and replacing the stitch on the left needle, insert the left needle from back to front, then knit this stitch through the back leg; purl 2, change the legs, before working the 2nd purl stitch, moving the back leg to the front, insert the right needle through the stitch from back to front, releasing the left needle from the stitch and replacing it on the left needle, then purl through the front leg now in front of the left needle* repeat from * to * until the end of the row before the edge stitch, knit 1 through the back leg.

Row 2: *Purl 2, change the legs before working the 2nd purl stitch, moving the back leg to the front; knit 2 through the back legs, before knitting the 2nd knit stitch, move the front leg of the 2nd knit stitch to the back as described in row 1* repeat from * to * until the end of the row before the edge stitch, purl 1.

Repeat rows: 1-2.

Bind off as follows: After the last row 2, turn your work over. The Front Side: slip all the stitches from the left needle to the right one; thus, the working yarn is at the end of the row; turn your work over. The Back Side: slip 2 purlwise from the left needle to the right one, insert the left needle through the front leg of the 1st slipped stitch from left to right, and pass it over the 2nd stitch (now there is 1 stitch on the right needle) *slip 1 purlwise from the left needle to the right one, insert the left needle through the front leg of the 1st stitch on the right needle from left to right and pass it over the 2nd stitch, now there is 1 stitch on the right needle* repeat from * to * until the end of the row.

Note: For trimming, bind off using larger needles than the working ones to create a larger chain of edge stitches, as this method of binding off creates a tight chain of edge stitches.

Pattern 24

Cast on a multiple of 3, plus 2 for symmetry and 2 edge stitches. Three-stitch repeat. Repeat rows: 1-4. The edge stitches are not included in the description below and must be added. Slip the first edge stitch, purl the last one.

Knit through the front legs, knit through the back leg, purl as if to purl in knitting through the back leg as follows: with the working yarn in front of the stitch, insert the right needle through the stitch from back to front, move the working yarn under the right needle, and pull it with the needle through the stitch. **Note:** The purl stitch that is worked this way sets up the knit stitch to be knitted through the back leg. **Knit tightly. Use a bulky yarn**.

Description:

Row 1 (Back Side): *Knit 2 through the back legs, yarn over forward (i.e., from yourself), with the working yarn behind your work, slip 1 purlwise* repeat from * to * until the end of the row before the edge stitch, knit 2 through the back legs.

Row 2: *Purl 2 as if to purl in knitting through the back legs, yarn over forward (i.e., from yourself), with the working yarn behind your work slip 1 stitch and yarn over purlwise* repeat from * to * until the end of the row before the edge stitch, purl 2 as if to purl in knitting through the back legs.

Row 3: *Knit 2 through the back legs, yarn over forward (i.e., from yourself), with the working yarn behind your work slip 1 stitch and 2 yarn overs purlwise* repeat from * to * until the end of the row before the edge stitch, knit 2 through the back legs.

Row 4: *Purl 2 as if to purl in knitting through the back legs, knit 1 together with 3 yarn overs through the front legs* repeat from * to * until the end of the row before the border stitch, purl 2 as if to purl in knitting through the back legs.

Repeat rows: 1-4.

Bind off as follows: After the last row 4, turn your work over. The Front Side: slip all the stitches from the left needle to the right one; thus, the working yarn is at the end of the row; turn your work over. The Back Side: slip 2 purlwise from the left needle to the right one, insert the left needle through the front leg of the 1st slipped stitch from left to right, and pass it over the 2nd stitch (now there is 1 stitch on the right needle) *slip 1 purlwise from the left needle to the right one, insert the left needle through the front leg of the 1st stitch on the right needle from left to right and pass it over the 2nd stitch, now there is 1 stitch on the right needle* repeat from * to * until the end of the row.

Note: For trimming, bind off using larger needles than the working ones to create a larger chain of edge stitches, as this method of binding off creates a tight chain of edge stitches.

Pattern 25

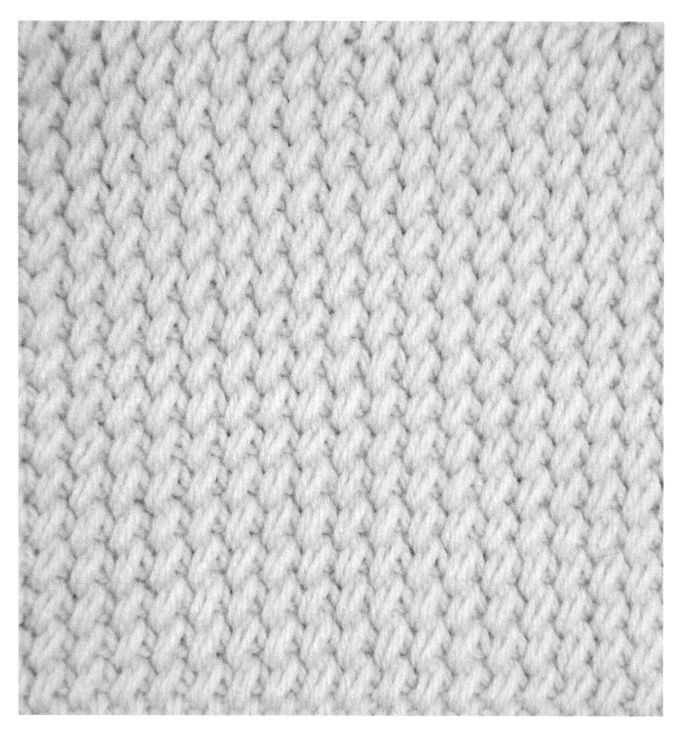

Cast on a multiple of 2, plus 1 and 2 edge stitches. Two-stitch repeat. Repeat rows: 3-4. The edge stitches are not included in the description below and must be added. Slip the first edge stitch, purl the last one.

Knit through the front leg, knit through the back leg, purl as follows: with the working yarn in front of the stitch, insert the right needle through the stitch from back to front, move the working yarn under the right needle, and pull it with the needle through the stitch. **Note:** The purl stitch that is worked this way sets up the knit stitch to be knitted through the back leg.

Description:

Row 1 (set up row): *knit 1 through the back leg, purl 1 as if to purl in knitting through the back leg* repeat from * to * until the end of the row before the edge stitch, knit 1 through the back leg.

Row 2 (set up row): *purl 1 as if to purl in knitting through the back leg, knit 1 through the back leg* repeat from * to * until the end of the row before the edge stitch, purl 1 as if to knit through the back leg.

Row 3: *Knit 2 as follows: with the working yarn behind your work, insert the right needle through the 2nd stitch 1 row below the stitch that is on the left needle, pull the working yarn onto the Front Side, and leave this stitch on the right needle, yarn over forward (i.e., from yourself), then knit 2 together through the front legs* repeat from * to * until the end of the row before the edge stitch, knit 1 through the back leg.

Row 4: *purl 2 together as if to purl in knitting through the back legs, knit 1 through the front leg* repeat from * to * until the end of the row before the edge stitch, knit 1 through the back leg.

Repeat rows: 3-4.

Bind off as follows: After the last row 4, turn your work over. The Front Side: slip all the stitches from the left needle to the right one; thus, the working yarn is at the end of the row; turn your work over. The Back Side: slip 2 purlwise from the left needle to the right one, insert the left needle through the front leg of the 1st slipped stitch from left to right, and pass it over the 2nd stitch (now there is 1 stitch on the right needle) *slip 1 purlwise from the left needle to the right one, insert the left needle through the front leg of the 1st stitch on the right needle from left to right and pass it over the 2nd stitch, now there is 1 stitch on the right needle* repeat from * to * until the end of the row.

Note: For trimming, bind off using larger needles than the working ones to create a larger chain of edge stitches, as this method of binding off creates a tight chain of edge stitches.

Pattern 26

Reversible

The Front Side   **The Back Side**

Cast on a multiple of 2, plus 1 for symmetry and 2 edge stitches. Two-stitch repeat. Repeat rows: 2-3. The edge stitches are not included in the description below and must be added. Slip the first edge stitch, purl the last one as if to knit through the back leg as follows: with the working yarn in front of the stitch, insert the right needle through the stitch from back to front, move the working yarn under the right needle, and pull it with the needle through the stitch. **Knit through the front legs. Use a bulky yarn.**

Description:

Row 1 (set up row): Knit all the stitches.

Row 2: *Knit 1, inserting the right needle through the stitch of the previous row (i.e., under the stitch that is on the left needle), knit the next 1* repeat from * to * until the end of the row before the edge stitch, knit 1, inserting the right needle through the stitch of the previous row.

Row 3: *Knit 1, knit the next 1, inserting the right needle through the stitch of the previous row* repeat from * to * until the end of the row before the edge stitch, knit 1.

Repeat rows: 2-3.

Bind off as follows: After the last row 3, turn your work over. The Front Side: slip all the stitches from the left needle to the right one; thus, the working yarn is at the end of the row; turn your work over. The Back Side: slip 2 purlwise from the left needle to the right one, insert the left needle through the front leg of the 1st slipped stitch from left to right, and pass it over the 2nd stitch (now there is 1 stitch on the right needle) *slip 1 purlwise from the left needle to the right one, insert the left needle through the front leg of the 1st stitch on the right needle from left to right and pass it over the 2nd stitch, now there is 1 stitch on the right needle* repeat from * to * until the end of the row.

Note: For trimming, bind off using larger needles than the working ones to create a larger chain of edge stitches, as this method of binding off creates a tight chain of edge stitches.

Pattern 27

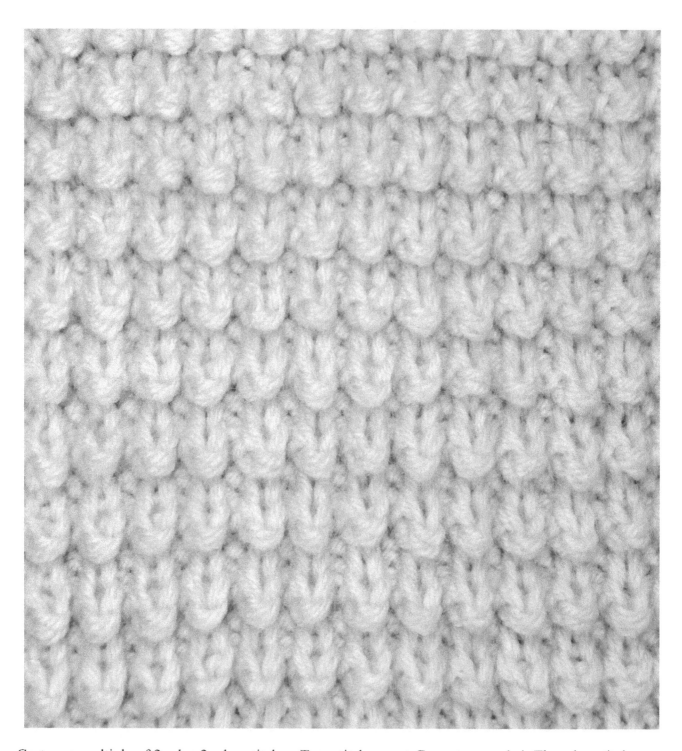

Cast on a multiple of 2, plus 2 edge stitches. Two-stitch repeat. Repeat rows: 1-4. The edge stitches are not included in the description below and must be added. **Knit the first edge stitch; knit the last edge stitch.**

Knit through the front leg, purl as follows: with the working yarn in front of the stitch, insert the right needle through the stitch from back to front, wrap the working yarn forward (i.e., from yourself) around the tip of the right needle, then pull the working yarn with the needle through the stitch. **Note:** The purl stitch that is worked this way sets up the knit stitch to be knitted through the front leg. **Knit tightly. Use a bulky yarn.**

Description:

Row 1 (Back Side): *Knit 1 through the front leg as follows: insert the right needle through the stitch from back to front and slip it onto the right needle, return it onto the left needle, inserting the left needle through the stitch straight, from left to right, now knit this stitch through the front leg, purl 1* repeat from * to * until the end of the row.

Row 2 (Front Side): *Knit 1, yarn over forward (i.e., from yourself), with the working yarn behind your work slip 1 purlwise* repeat from * to * until the end of the row.

Row 3 (Back Side): *Yarn over forward (i.e., from yourself), with the working yarn behind your work slip 1 stitch and yarn over of the previous row purlwise, then knit 1* repeat from * to * until the end of the row.

Row 4 (Front Side): *Knit 1, purl 1 together with 2 yarn overs of the previous rows as if to purl in knitting through the back leg as follows: with the working yarn in front of these 3 stitches, insert the right needle through them from back to front, then move the working yarn under the right needle and pull it with the right needle through these 3 stitches* repeat from * to * until the end of the row.

Repeat rows: 1-4.

Bind off after the last row 1 as follows: slip the edge stitch onto the right needle, knit the next 1 through the front leg, then insert the left needle through the slipped edge stitch from left to right and pass it over the knitted stitch, *now there is 1 stitch on the right needle, knit the next 1 through the front leg (now there are 2 stitches on the right needle), insert the left needle through the 1st stitch on the right needle from left to right and pass it over the 2nd stitch* repeat from * to * until the end of the row.

Pattern 28

Reversible

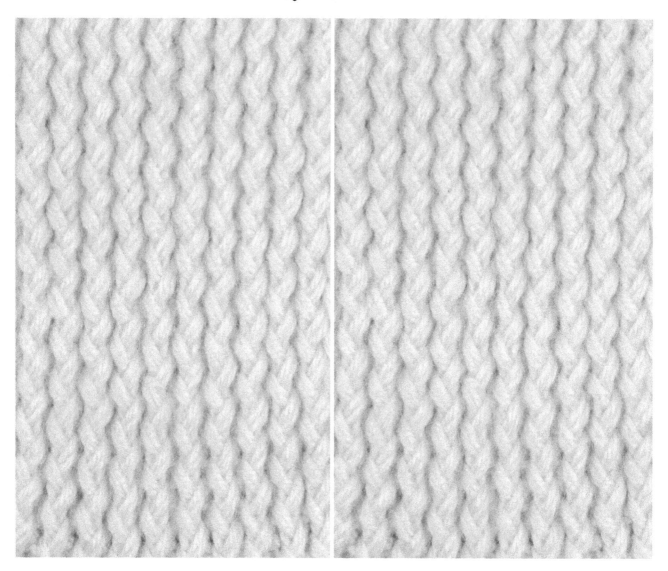

The Front Side   **The Back Side**

Cast on a multiple of 2, plus 2 edge stitches. Two-stitch repeat. Repeat row 1.

The edge stitches are not included in the description below and must be added. Slip the first edge stitch, purl the last one as if to purl in knitting through the back leg as follows: with the working yarn in front of the stitch, insert the right needle through the stitch from back to front, move the working yarn under the right needle, and pull it with the needle through the stitch. **Use a bulky yarn.**

Description:

Row 1: *Knit 1 through the back leg as follows: with the working yarn behind your work, insert the right needle through the stitch from front to back the needle must be under the working yarn in the direction going up, then wrap the working yarn backward (i.e., to yourself) around the needle and pull it through the stitch, **purl 1 as follows:** with the working yarn in front of the stitch, insert the right needle through the stitch from back to front and wrap the working yarn forward (i.e., from yourself) around the tip of the right needle, then pull the working yarn with the right needle through the stitch. **Note:** The purl stitch that is worked this way sets up the knit stitch to be knitted through the front leg* repeat from * to * until the end of the row.

Repeat row 1.

Bind off as follows: After the last row, turn your work over. The Front Side: slip all the stitches from the left needle to the right one; thus, the working yarn is at the end of the row; turn your work over. The Back Side: slip 2 purlwise from the left needle to the right one, insert the left needle through the front leg of the 1st slipped stitch from left to right, and pass it over the 2nd stitch (now there is 1 stitch on the right needle) *slip 1 purlwise from the left needle to the right one, insert the left needle through the front leg of the 1st stitch on the right needle from left to right and pass it over the 2nd stitch, now there is 1 stitch on the right needle* repeat from * to * until the end of the row.

Note: For trimming, bind off using larger needles than the working ones to create a larger chain of edge stitches, as this method of binding off creates a tight chain of edge stitches.

Pattern 29

Cast on a multiple of 3, plus 1 for symmetry and 2 edge stitches. Three-stitch repeat. Repeat rows: 1-2. The edge stitches are not included in the description below and must be added. Slip the first edge stitch, purl the last one.

Knit through the back leg, purl as follows: with the working yarn in front of the stitch, insert the right needle through the stitch from back to front, move the working yarn under the right needle, and pull it with the needle through the stitch. **Note:** The purl stitch that is worked this way sets up the knit stitch to be knitted through the back leg.

Description:

Row 1: *Purl 1, knit 2 as follows: knit the 2nd stitch through the back leg, then knit the 1st stitch through the back leg* repeat from * to * until the end of the row before the edge stitch, purl 1.

Row 2: *Knit 1, purl 2 as follows: purl the 2nd stitch, then purl the 1st stitch* repeat from * to * until the end of the row before the edge stitch, knit 1.

Repeat rows: 1-2.

Bind off as follows: After the last row 2, turn your work over. The Front Side: slip all the stitches from the left needle to the right one; thus, the working yarn is at the end of the row; turn your work over. The Back Side: slip 2 purlwise from the left needle to the right one, insert the left needle through the front leg of the 1st slipped stitch from left to right, and pass it over the 2nd stitch (now there is 1 stitch on the right needle) *slip 1 purlwise from the left needle to the right one, insert the left needle through the front leg of the 1st stitch on the right needle from left to right and pass it over the 2nd stitch, now there is 1 stitch on the right needle* repeat from * to * until the end of the row.

Note: For trimming, bind off using larger needles than the working ones to create a larger chain of edge stitches, as this method of binding off creates a tight chain of edge stitches.

Pattern 30

Reversible

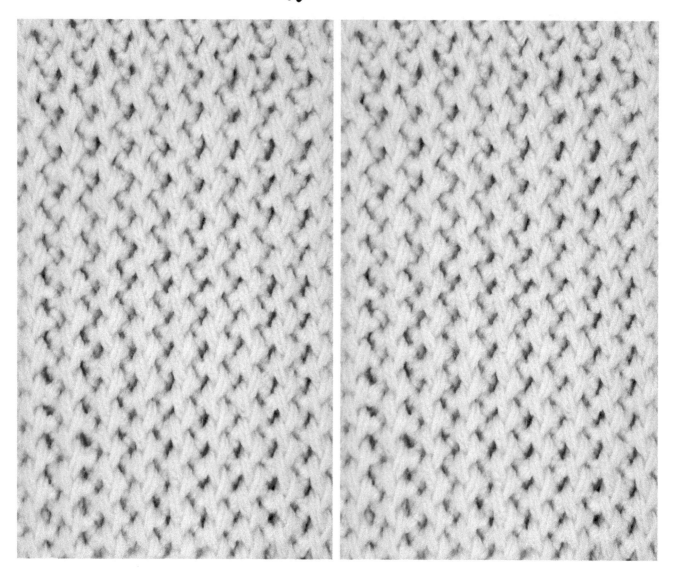

| **The Front Side** | **The Back Side** |

Cast on a multiple of 4, plus 2 for symmetry and 2 edge stitches. Four-stitch repeat. Repeat rows: 1-2. The edge stitches are not included in the description below and must be added. Slip the first edge stitch, purl the last one.

Knit through the back leg, purl as follows: with the working yarn in front of the stitch, insert the right needle through the stitch from back to front, move the working yarn under the right needle, and pull it with the needle through the stitch. **Note:** The purl stitch that is worked this way sets up the knit stitch to be knitted through the back leg. **Use a bulky yarn.**

Description:

Row 1: *Purl 2 as follows: purl the 2nd stitch and leave it on the left needle, then purl the 1st stitch; knit 2 as follows: knit the 2nd stitch through the back leg and leave it on the left needle, then knit the 1st stitch through the back leg* repeat from * to * until the end of the row before the edge stitch, purl 2 as follows: purl the 2nd stitch and leave it on the left needle, then purl the 1st stitch.

Row 2: *Knit 2 as follows: knit the 2nd stitch through the back leg and leave it on the left needle, then knit the 1st stitch through the back leg; purl 2 as follows: purl the 2nd stitch and leave it on the left needle, then purl the 1st stitch* repeat from * to * until the end of the row before the edge stitch, knit 2 as follows: knit the 2nd stitch through the back leg and leave it on the left needle, then knit the 1st stitch through the back leg.

Repeat rows: 1-2.

Bind off as follows: After the last row 2, turn your work over. The Front Side: slip all the stitches from the left needle to the right one; thus, the working yarn is at the end of the row; turn your work over. The Back Side: slip 2 purlwise from the left needle to the right one, insert the left needle through the front leg of the 1st slipped stitch from left to right, and pass it over the 2nd stitch (now there is 1 stitch on the right needle) *slip 1 purlwise from the left needle to the right one, insert the left needle through the front leg of the 1st stitch on the right needle from left to right and pass it over the 2nd stitch, now there is 1 stitch on the right needle* repeat from * to * until the end of the row.

Note: For trimming, bind off using larger needles than the working ones to create a larger chain of edge stitches, as this method of binding off creates a tight chain of edge stitches.

Pattern 31

Horizontal ribbing

The Front Side

The Back Side

Cast on a multiple of 2, plus 1 and 2 edge stitches. Two-stitch repeat. Repeat rows: 1-4. The edge stitches are not included in the description below and must be added. Slip the first edge stitch, purl the last one as if to knit through the back leg as follows: with the working yarn in front of the stitch, insert the right needle through the stitch from back to front, move the working yarn under the right needle, and pull it with the needle through the stitch.

Knit through the front leg, purl as follows: with the working yarn in front of the stitch, insert the right needle through the stitch from back to front, wrap the working yarn forward (i.e., from yourself) around the tip of the right needle, then pull the working yarn with the needle through the stitch. **Note:** The purl stitch that is worked this way sets up the knit stitch to be knitted through the front leg.

Note: This pattern has a stretchy texture.

Description:

Row 1: *Purl 1, with the working yarn in front of your work slip 1 purlwise* repeat from * to * until the end of the row before the edge stitch, purl 1.

Row 2: *With the working yarn behind your work, slip 1 purlwise, knit 1* repeat from * to * until the end of the row before the edge stitch, with the working yarn behind your work slip 1 purlwise.

Row 3: Knit all the stitches.

Row 4: Purl all the stitches.

Repeat rows: 1-4.

Bind off as follows: After the last row 1, turn your work over. The Back Side: slip all the stitches from the left needle to the right one; thus, the working yarn is at the end of the row; turn your work over. The Front Side: slip 2 purlwise from the left needle to the right one, insert the left needle through the front leg of the 1st slipped stitch from left to right, and pass it over the 2nd stitch (now there is 1 stitch on the right needle) *slip 1 purlwise from the left needle to the right one, insert the left needle through the front leg of the 1st stitch on the right needle from left to right and pass it over the 2nd stitch, now there is 1 stitch on the right needle* repeat from * to * until the end of the row.

Note: For trimming, bind off using larger needles than the working ones to create a larger chain of edge stitches, as this method of binding off creates a tight chain of edge stitches.

Pattern 32

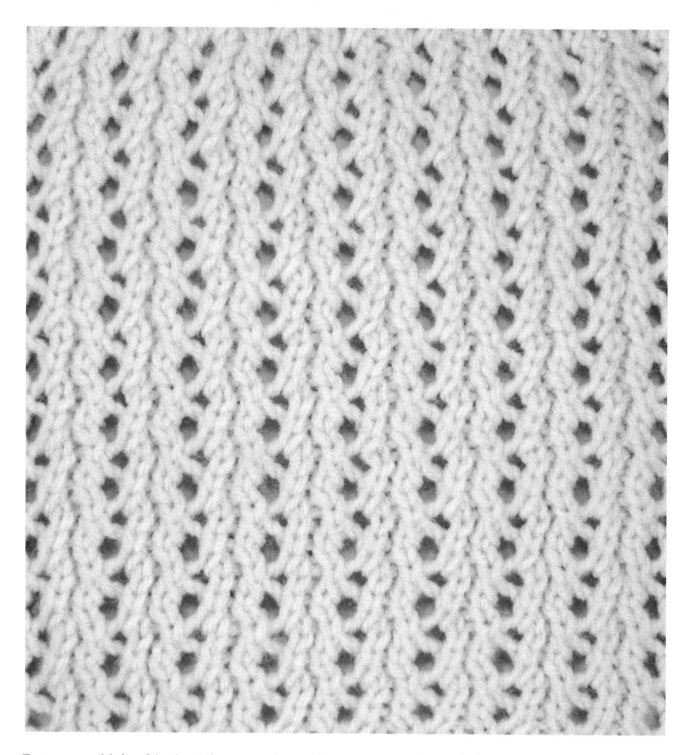

Cast on a multiple of 4, plus 1 for symmetry and 2 edge stitches. Four-stitch repeat. Repeat rows: 1-4. The edge stitches are not included in the description below and must be added. Slip the first edge stitch, purl the last one as if to purl in knitting through the back leg as follows: with the working yarn in front of the stitch, insert the right needle through the stitch from back to front, move the working yarn under the right needle, and pull it with the needle through the stitch.

Knit through the front leg, purl as follows: with the working yarn in front of the stitch, insert the right needle through the stitch from back to front, wrap the working yarn forward (i.e., from yourself) around the tip of the right needle, then pull the working yarn with the right needle through the stitch. **Note:** The purl stitch that is worked this way sets up the knit stitch to be knitted through the front leg. **Knit tightly.**

Description:

Row 1: *Purl 1, knit 1, yarn over forward (i.e., from yourself), knit 2 together through the back legs as follows: insert the right needle through the front leg of the 1st stitch from front to back and slip it onto the right needle, then insert the right needle through the front leg of the 2nd stitch from front to back and slip it onto the right needle, return both stitches onto the left needle, then knit 2 together through the back legs* repeat from * to * until the end of the row before the edge stitch, purl 1.

Row 2: *Knit 1, purl 3* repeat from * to * until the end of the row, before the edge stitch, knit 1.

Row 3: *Purl 1, knit 2 together through the front legs, yarn over forward (i.e., from yourself), knit 1* repeat from * to * until the end of the row before the edge stitch, purl 1.

Row 4: * Knit 1, purl 3* repeat from * to * until the end of the row before the edge stitch, knit 1.

Repeat rows: 1-4.

Bind off after the last row 4 as follows: Slip the edge stitch onto the right needle, knit the next 1, then insert the left needle through the slipped edge stitch from left to right and pass it over the knitted stitch, *now there is 1 stitch on the right needle, knit the next 1, insert the left needle through the 1st stitch on the right needle from left to right and pass it over the 2nd stitch* repeat from * to * until the end of the row.

Pattern 33

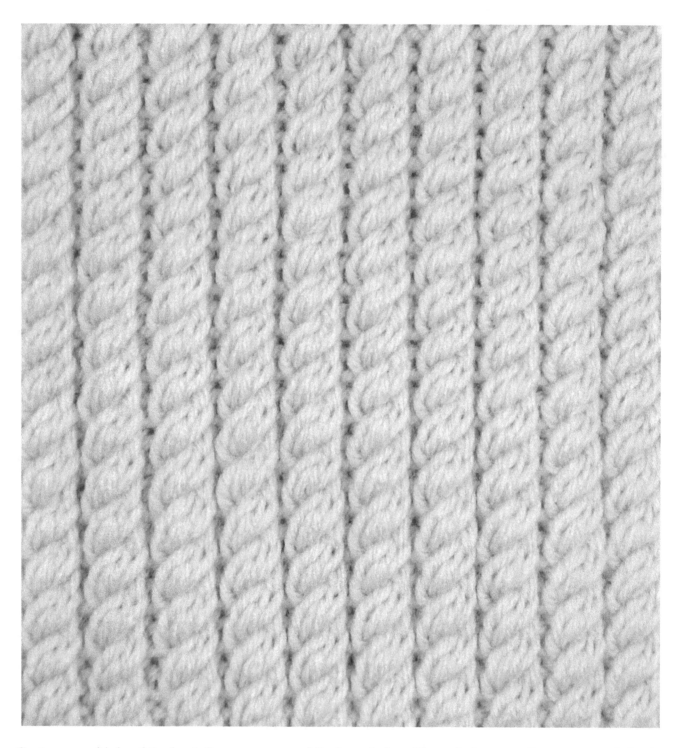

Cast on a multiple of 5, plus 1 for symmetry and 2 edge stitches. Five-stitch repeat. Repeat rows: 1-2. The edge stitches are not included in the description below and must be added. Slip the first edge stitch, purl the last one.

Knit through the back leg, purl as follows: with the working yarn in front of the stitch, insert the right needle through the stitch from back to front, move the working yarn under the right needle, and pull it with the needle through the stitch. **Note:** The purl stitch that is worked this way sets up the knit stitch to be knitted through the back leg.

Description:

Row 1: *Purl 1, slip 2 onto a cable needle behind your work, knit the next 2, then knit the slipped 2* repeat from * to * before the edge stitch, purl 1.

Row 2: *Knit 1, purl 4* repeat from * to * before the edge stitch, knit 1.

Repeat rows: 1-2.

Bind off as follows: After the last row 1, turn your work over. The Back Side: slip all the stitches from the left needle to the right one; thus, the working yarn is at the end of the row; turn your work over. The Front Side: slip 2 purlwise from the left needle to the right one, insert the left needle through the front leg of the 1st slipped stitch from left to right, and pass it over the 2nd stitch (now there is 1 stitch on the right needle) *slip 1 purlwise from the left needle to the right one, insert the left needle through the front leg of the 1st stitch on the right needle from left to right and pass it over the 2nd stitch, now there is 1 stitch on the right needle* repeat from * to * until the end of the row.

Note: For trimming, bind off using larger needles than the working ones to create a larger chain of edge stitches, as this method of binding off creates a tight chain of edge stitches.

Pattern 34

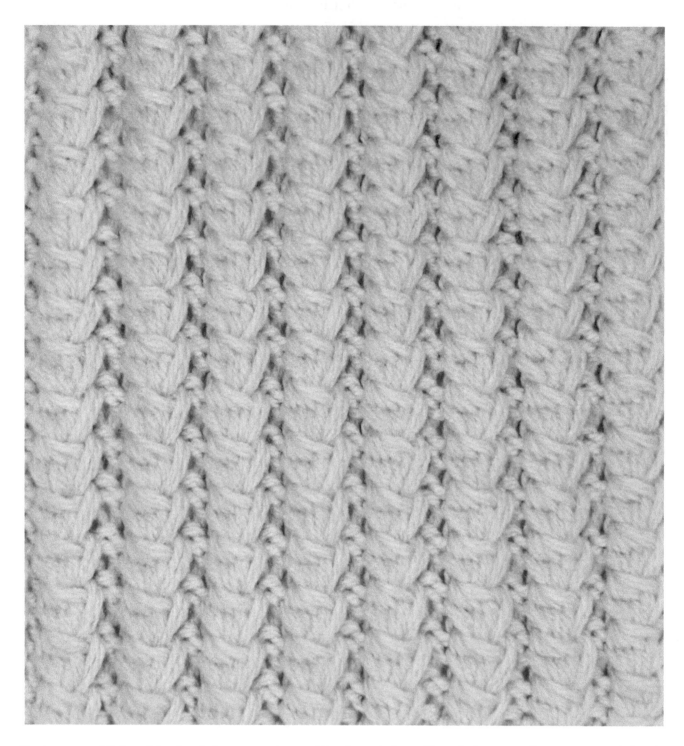

Cast on a multiple of 6, plus 1 for symmetry and 2 edge stitches. Six-stitch repeat. Repeat rows: 1-2. The edge stitches are not included in the description below and must be added. Slip the first edge stitch, purl the last one.

Knit through the back leg, purl as follows: with the working yarn in front of the stitch, insert the right needle through the stitch from back to front, move the working yarn under the right needle, and pull it with the needle through the stitch. **Note:** The purl stitch that is worked this way sets up the knit stitch to be knitted through the back leg.

Description:

Row 1: *Purl 1, knit 5 out of 5 as follows: knit 5 stitches together through the back legs—do not release the left needle yet—yarn over forward (i.e., from yourself), knit these 5 stitches together 1 more time, make 1 more yarn over forward (i.e., from yourself), knit these 5 stitches together 1 more time* repeat from * to * until the end of the row before the edge stitch, purl 1.

Row 2: *Knit 1 through the back leg, purl 5* repeat from * to * until the end of the row before the edge stitch, knit 1 through the back leg.

Repeat rows: 1-2.

Bind off as follows: After the last row 2, turn your work over. The Front Side: slip all the stitches from the left needle to the right one; thus, the working yarn is at the end of the row; turn your work over. The Back Side: slip 2 purlwise from the left needle to the right one, insert the left needle through the front leg of the 1st slipped stitch from left to right, and pass it over the 2nd stitch (now there is 1 stitch on the right needle) *slip 1 purlwise from the left needle to the right one, insert the left needle through the front leg of the 1st stitch on the right needle from left to right and pass it over the 2nd stitch, now there is 1 stitch on the right needle* repeat from * to * until the end of the row.

Note: For trimming, bind off using larger needles than the working ones to create a larger chain of edge stitches, as this method of binding off creates a tight chain of edge stitches.

Pattern 35

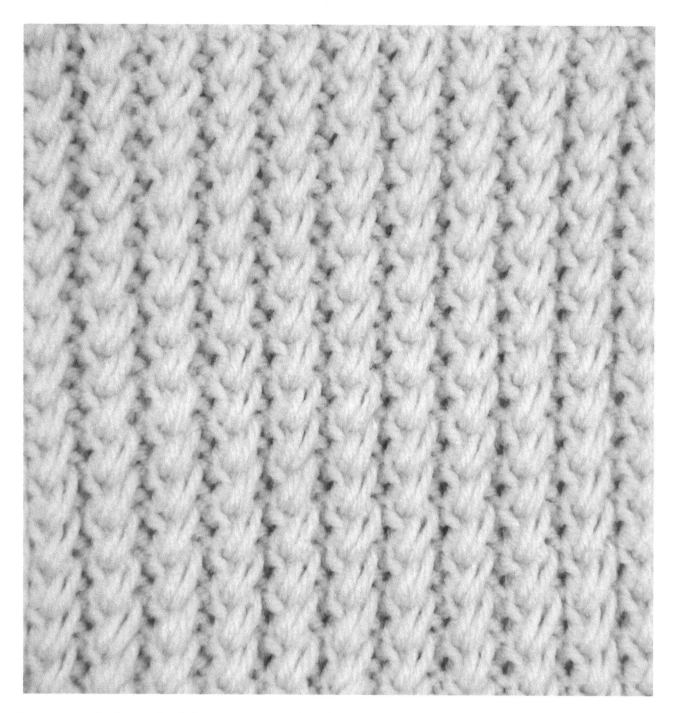

Cast on a multiple 4, plus 1 for symmetry and 2 edge stitches. Four-stitch repeat. Repeat rows: 1-2. The edge stitches are not included in the description below and must be added. Slip the first edge stitch, purl the last one.

Knit through the back leg, purl as follows: with the working yarn in front of the stitch, insert the right needle through the stitch from back to front, move the working yarn under the right needle, and pull it with

the needle through the stitch. **Note:** The purl stitch that is worked this way sets up the knit stitch to be knitted through the back leg.

Description:

Row 1: *Purl 1, knit 3 as follows: with the working yarn behind your work, insert the right needle from front to back into space between the 2nd and 3rd stitches, pull the working yarn through, and leave a loop on the right needle, make 1 yarn over forward (i.e., from yourself), then knit these 3 stitches on the left needle together through the back legs* repeat from * to * until the end of the row before the edge stitch, purl 1.

Row 2: *Knit 1, purl 3* repeat from * to * until the end of the row before the edge stitch, knit 1.

Repeat rows: 1-2.

Bind off as follows: After the last row 2, turn your work over. The Front Side: slip all the stitches from the left needle to the right one; thus, the working yarn is at the end of the row; turn your work over. The Back Side: slip 2 purlwise from the left needle to the right one, insert the left needle through the front leg of the 1st slipped stitch from left to right, and pass it over the 2nd stitch (now there is 1 stitch on the right needle) *slip 1 purlwise from the left needle to the right one, insert the left needle through the front leg of the 1st stitch on the right needle from left to right and pass it over the 2nd stitch, now there is 1 stitch on the right needle* repeat from * to * until the end of the row.

Note: For trimming, bind off using larger needles than the working ones to create a larger chain of edge stitches, as this method of binding off creates a tight chain of edge stitches.

Pattern 36

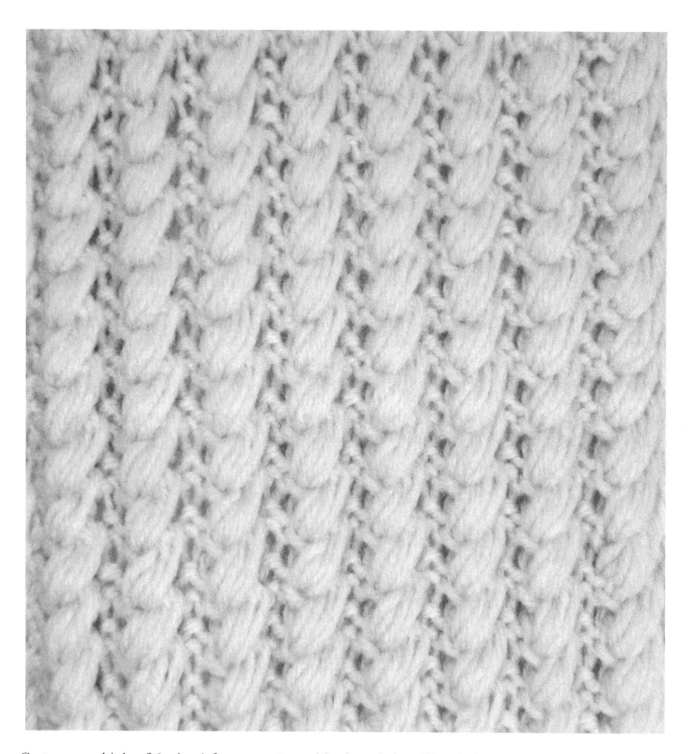

Cast on a multiple of 6, plus 1 for symmetry and 2 edge stitches. Six-stitch repeat. Repeat rows: 1-2. The edge stitches are not included in the description below and must be added. Slip the first edge stitch, purl the last one.

Knit through the back leg, purl as follows: with the working yarn in front of the stitch, insert the right needle through the stitch from back to front, move the working yarn under the right needle, and pull it with the needle through the stitch. **Note:** The purl stitch that is worked this way sets up the knit stitch to be knitted through the back leg.

Description:

Row 1: *Purl 1, knit 5 as follows: with the working yarn behind your work, insert the right needle from front to back between the 4th and 5th stitches, pull the working yarn through and leave a loop on the right needle, yarn over forward (i.e., from yourself), then insert the right needle between the 4th and 5th stitches 1 more time, pull the working yarn through and leave a loop on the right needle, yarn over forward (i.e., from yourself), then knit these 5 stitches on the left needle together through the back legs* repeat from * to *until the end of the row before the edge stitch, purl 1.

Row 2: *Knit 1, purl 5* repeat from * to * until the end of the row before the edge stitch, knit 1.

Repeat rows: 1-2.

Bind off as follows: After the last row 2, turn your work over. The Front Side: slip all the stitches from the left needle to the right one; thus, the working yarn is at the end of the row; turn your work over. The Back Side: slip 2 purlwise from the left needle to the right one, insert the left needle through the front leg of the 1st slipped stitch from left to right, and pass it over the 2nd stitch (now there is 1 stitch on the right needle) *slip 1 purlwise from the left needle to the right one, insert the left needle through the front leg of the 1st stitch on the right needle from left to right and pass it over the 2nd stitch, now there is 1 stitch on the right needle* repeat from * to * until the end of the row.

Note: For trimming, bind off using larger needles than the working ones to create a larger chain of edge stitches, as this method of binding off creates a tight chain of edge stitches.

Pattern 37

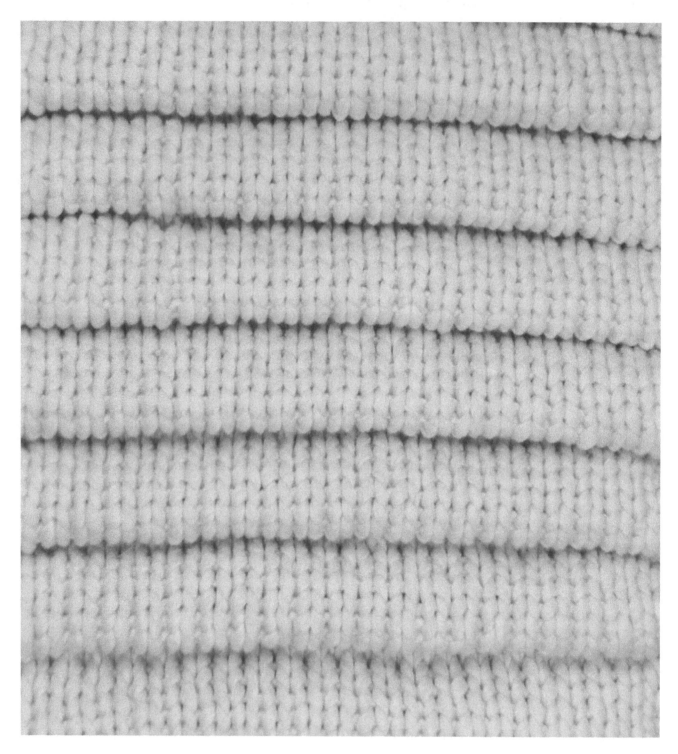

Cast on a multiple of 2, plus 1 and 2 edge stitches. Two-stitch repeat. Repeat rows: 1-12.

The edge stitches are not included in the description below and must be added. Slip the first edge stitch, purl the last one.

Knit through the back leg, purl as follows: with the working yarn in front of the stitch, insert the right needle through the stitch from back to front, move the working yarn under the right needle, and pull it with the needle through the stitch. **Note:** The purl stitch that is worked this way sets up the knit stitch to be knitted through the back leg. **Needles: 3 mm. Use a bulky yarn.**

Description:

Row 1: *Knit 1, with the working yarn in front of the stitch slip 1* repeat from * to * until the end of the row before the edge stitch, knit 1.

Row 2: *Purl 1, with the working yarn behind the stitch slip 1* repeat from * to * until the end of the row before the edge stitch, purl 1.

Row 3: Repeat row 1.

Row 4: Repeat row 2.

Row 5: Repeat row 1.

Row 6: Repeat row 2.

Row 7: Repeat row 1.

Row 8: Repeat row 2.

Row 9: Repeat row 1.

Row 10: Purl all the stitches.

Row 11: Knit all the stitches.

Row 12: Purl all the stitches.

Repeat rows: 1-12.

Bind off as follows: Slip the edge stitch onto the right needle, knit the next 1, then insert the left needle through the slipped edge stitch from left to right and pass it over the knitted one; *now there is 1 stitch on the right needle, knit the next 1 (now there are 2 stitches on the right needle), insert the left needle through the 1st stitch on the right needle from left to right and pass it over the 2nd one* repeat from * to * until the end of the row.

Pattern 38

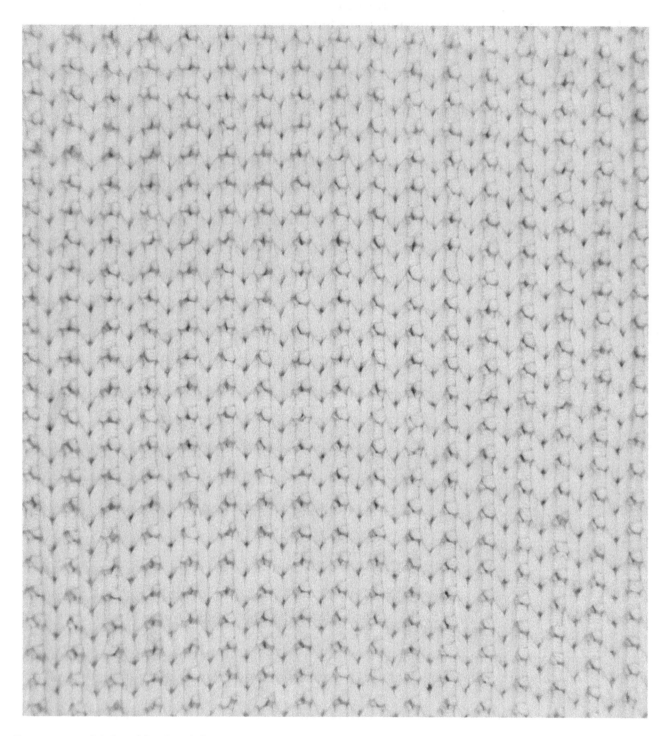

Cast on a multiple of 2, plus 1 for symmetry and 2 edge stitches. Two-stitch repeat. Repeat rows: 1-2. The edge stitches are not included in the description below and must be added. Slip the first edge stitch, purl the last one as if to purl in knitting through the back leg as follows: with the working yarn in front of the stitch, insert the right needle through the stitch from back to front, move the working yarn under the right needle, and pull it with the needle through the stitch.

Knit through the front leg, purl as follows: with the working yarn in front of the stitch, insert the right needle through the stitch from back to front, wrap the working yarn forward (i.e., from yourself) around the tip of the right needle, then pull the working yarn with the needle through the stitch. **Note:** The purl stitch that is worked this way sets up the knit stitch to be knitted through the front leg. **Needles: 2.5 mm. Knit tightly. Use a bulky yarn.**

Description:

Row 1: *Purl 1, with the working yarn behind your work slip 1* repeat from * to * until the end of the row before the edge stitch, purl 1.

Row 2: Purl all the stitches.

Repeat rows: 1-2.

Bind off as follows: Slip the edge stitch onto the right needle, purl the next 1, insert the left needle through the 1st stitch on the right needle from left to right, and pass it over the 2nd one (now there is 1 stitch on the right needle); *knit 1, insert the left needle through the 1st stitch on the right needle from left to right and pass it over the 2nd one (now there is 1 stitch on the right needle), bind off the next 4 (knit stitches) the same as the 1st knit stitch, then purl 1, insert the left needle through the 1st stitch on the right needle from left to right and pass it over the 2nd one (now there is 1 stitch on the right needle)* repeat from * to * until the end of the row, purl the edge stitch, insert the left needle through the 1st stitch on the right needle from left to right and pass it over the 2nd one.

Pattern 39

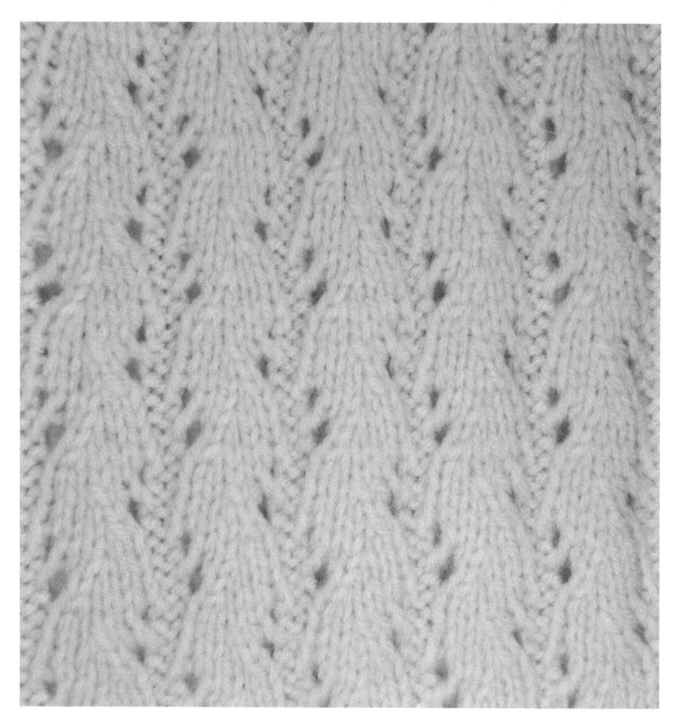

Cast on a multiple of 7, plus 2 for symmetry and 2 edge stitches. Seven-stitch repeat. Repeat rows: 1-8. The edge stitches are not included in the description below and must be added. **Slip the first edge stitch; purl the last edge one.**

Knit through the back leg, purl as follows: with the working yarn in front of the stitch, insert the right needle through the stitch from back to front, move the working yarn under the right needle and pull it with the needle through the stitch. The purl stitch that is worked this way sets up the knit stitch to be knitted through the back leg. **Needles: 2.5 mm.**

Description:

Row 1: *Purl 2, knit 3, knit the next 2 together through the front legs as follows: slip 1 purlwise onto the right needle, insert the right needle through the 2nd stitch from back to front and slip it onto the right needle, thus moving the back leg to the front, return both stitches onto the left needle, now knit 2 together through the front legs, then yarn over forward (i.e., from yourself)* repeat from * to * until the end of the row before the edge stitch, purl 2.

Row 2: *Knit 2, purl 5* repeat from * to * until the end of the row before the edge stitch, knit 2.

Row 3: *Purl 2, knit 2, knit 2 together as described in row 1, knit the next 1, yarn over forward (i.e., from yourself)* repeat from * to * until the end of the row before the edge stitch, purl 2.

Row 4: *Knit 2, purl 5* repeat from * to * until the end of the row before the edge stitch, knit 2.

Row 5: *Purl 2, yarn over forward (i.e., from yourself), knit 2 together through the back legs as follows: slip the 1st stitch purlwise onto the right needle, insert the right needle through the 2nd stitch from back to front and slip it onto the right needle, thus moving the back leg to the front, return both stitches onto the left needle, now knit 2 together through the back legs, knit the next 3* repeat from * to * until the end of the row before the edge stitch, purl 2.

Row 6: *Knit 2, purl 6* repeat from * to * until the end of the row before the edge stitch, knit 2.

Row 7: *Purl 2, yarn over forward, knit 1, knit 2 together through the back legs as described in row 5, knit 2* repeat from * to * until the end of the row before the edge stitch, purl 2.

Row 8: *Knit 2, purl 5* repeat from * to * until the end of the row before the edge stitch, knit 2.

Repeat rows: 1-8.

Bind off as follows: Slip the edge stitch onto the right needle, knit the next 1, then insert the left needle through the slipped edge stitch from left to right and pass it over the knitted one, *now there is 1 stitch on the right needle, *knit the next 1 (now there are 2 stitches on the right needle), insert the left needle through the 1st stitch on the right needle from left to right and pass it over the 2nd one* repeat from * to * until the end of the row.

Pattern 40

Reversible

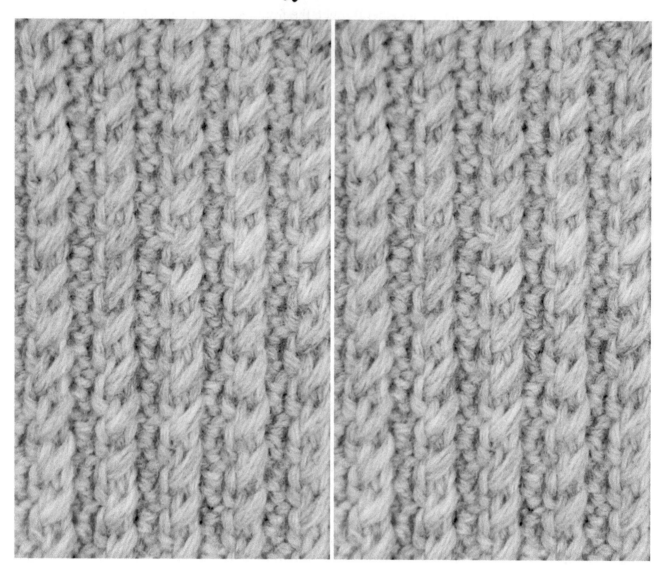

The Front Side   **The Back Side**

Cast on a multiple of 4, plus 2 for symmetry and 2 edge stitches. Four-stitch repeat. Repeat rows: 1-2. The edge stitches are not included in the description below and must be added. Slip the first edge stitch, purl the last one.

Knit through the front leg, knit through the back leg, purl as follows: with the working yarn in front of the stitch, insert the right needle through the stitch from back to front, then move the working yarn under the right needle and pull it with the needle through the stitch. **Note:** The purl stitch that is worked this way sets up the knit stitch to be knitted through the back leg. **Use a bulky yarn.**

Description:

Row 1: *Purl 2, knit 2 as follows: knit the 2nd of the 2 stitches through the front leg, then knit the 1st stitch through the back leg* repeat from * to * until the end of the row before the edge stitch, purl 2.

Row 2: *Knit 2 as follows: knit the 2nd stitch through the front leg, then knit the 1st stitch through the back leg, purl 2* repeat from * to * until the end of the row before the edge stitch, knit 2 as described above.

Repeat rows: 1-2.

Bind off as follows: After the last row 2, turn your work over. The Front Side: slip all the stitches from the left needle to the right one; thus, the working yarn is at the end of the row, then turn your work over. The Back Side: slip 2 purlwise from the left needle to the right one, insert the left needle through the front leg of the 1st slipped stitch from left to right, and pass it over the 2nd stitch (now there is 1 stitch on the right needle) *slip 1 purlwise from the left needle to the right one, insert the left needle through the front leg of the 1st stitch on the right needle from left to right and pass it over the 2nd stitch, now there is 1 stitch on the right needle* repeat from * to * until the end of the row.

Note: For trimming, bind off using larger needles than the working ones to create a larger chain of edge stitches, as this method of binding off creates a tight chain of edge stitches.

Pattern 41

Cast on a multiple of 20, plus 2 for symmetry and 2 edge stitches. Twenty-stitch repeat. Repeat rows: 1-6. The edge stitches are not included in the description below and must be added. Slip the first edge stitch, purl the last one.

Knit through the back leg, purl as follows: with the working yarn in front of the stitch, insert the right needle through the stitch from back to front, move the working yarn under the needle, and pull it with the needle through the stitch. **Note:** The purl stitch that is worked this way sets up the knit stitch to be knitted through the back leg.

Description:

Row 1: *Purl 2, slip 3 onto a cable needle in front of your work, knit the next 3, then knit the slipped 3, knit 6, slip the next 3 onto a cable needle behind your work, knit the next 3, then knit the slipped 3* repeat from * to * until the end of the row before the edge stitch, purl 2.

Row 2: *Knit 2, purl 18* repeat from * to * until the end of the row before the edge stitch, knit 2.

Row 3: *Purl 2, knit 3, slip the next 3 onto a cable needle in front of your work, knit the next 3, then knit the slipped 3, slip the next 3 onto a cable needle behind of your work, knit the next 3, then knit the slipped 3, knit the next 3* repeat from * to * until the end of the row before the edge stitch, purl 2.

Row 4: *Knit 2, purl 18* repeat from * to * until the end of the row before the edge stitch, knit 2.

Row 5: *Purl 2, knit 6, slip the next 3 onto a cable needle in front of your work, knit the next 3, then knit the slipped 3, knit the next 6* repeat from * to * until the end of the row before the edge stitch, purl 2.

Row 6: *Knit 2, purl 18* repeat from * to * until the end of the row before the edge stitch, knit 2.

Repeat rows: 1-6.

Bind off as follows: After the last row 6, turn your work over. The Front Side: slip all the stitches from the left needle to the right one; thus, the working yarn is at the end of the row, then turn your work over. The Back Side: slip 2 purlwise from the left needle to the right one, insert the left needle through the front leg of the 1st slipped stitch from left to right, and pass it over the 2nd stitch (now there is 1 stitch on the right needle) *slip 1 purlwise from the left needle to the right one, insert the left needle through the front leg of the 1st stitch on the right needle from left to right and pass it over the 2nd stitch, now there is 1 stitch on the right needle* repeat from * to * until the end of the row.

Note: For trimming, bind off using larger needles than the working ones to create a larger chain of edge stitches, as this method of binding off creates a tight chain of edge stitches.

Pattern 42

Reversible

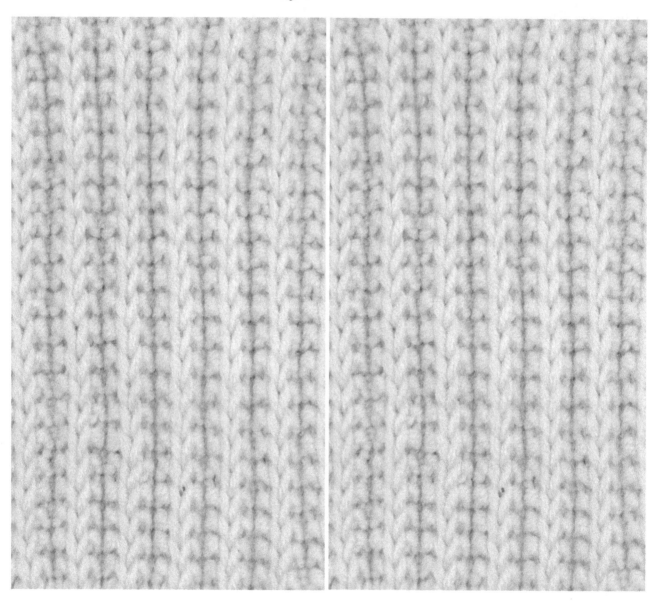

The Front Side   **The Back Side**

Cast on a multiple of 4, plus 3 for symmetry and 2 edge stitches. Four-stitch repeat. Repeat rows: 1-2. The edge stitches are not included in the description below and must be added. Slip the first edge stitch, purl the last one as if to purl in knitting through the back leg as follows: with the working yarn in front of the stitch, insert the right needle through the stitch from back to front, move the working yarn under the right needle, and pull it with the needle through the stitch.

Description:

Row 1: *Knit 3 through the front legs, with the working yarn in front of your work slip 1 stitch purlwise and return the working yarn to the back* repeat from * to * until the end of the row before the edge stitch, knit 3 through the front legs.

Row 2: Knit 1 through the front leg, *with the working yarn in front of your work, slip 1 stitch purlwise and return the working yarn to the back, knit 3 through the front legs* repeat from * to * until the end of the row before the edge stitch, with the working yarn in front your work, slip 1 purlwise and return the working yarn to the back, knit 1 through the front leg.

Repeat rows: 1-2.

Bind off as follows: After the last row 2, turn your work over. The Front Side: slip all the stitches from the left needle to the right one; thus, the working yarn is at the end of the row, then turn your work over. The Back Side: slip 2 purlwise from the left needle to the right one, insert the left needle through the front leg of the 1st slipped stitch from left to right, and pass it over the 2nd stitch (now there is 1 stitch on the right needle) *slip 1 purlwise from the left needle to the right one, insert the left needle through the front leg of the 1st stitch on the right needle from left to right and pass it over the 2nd stitch, now there is 1 stitch on the right needle* repeat from * to * until the end of the row.

Note: For trimming, bind off using larger needles than the working ones to create a larger chain of edge stitches, as this method of binding off creates a tight chain of edge stitches.

Pattern 43

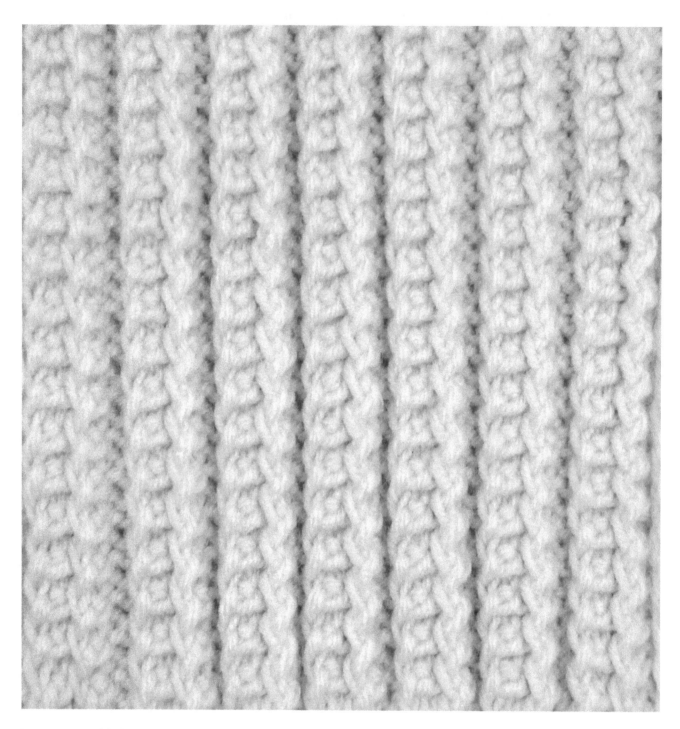

Cast on a multiple of 6, plus 2 for symmetry and 2 edge stitches. Six-stitch repeat. Repeat rows: 1-2. The edge stitches are not included in the description below and must be added. Slip the first edge stitch, purl the last one.

Knit through the front leg, knit through the back leg, purl as follows: with the working yarn in front of the stitch, insert the right needle through the stitch from back to front, then move the working yarn under the right needle and pull it with the needle through the stitch. **Note:** The purl stitch that is worked this way sets up the knit stitch to be knitted through the back leg.

Description:

Row 1: *Knit 2 through the back legs, yarn over forward (i.e., from yourself), knit 2 through the front legs, insert the left needle through the yarn over and pass it over these 2 knitted stitches, yarn over forward (i.e., from yourself), knit 2 through the front legs, insert the left needle through the yarn over and pass it over these 2 knitted stitches* repeat from * to * until the end of the row before the edge stitch, knit 2 through the back legs.

Row 2: *purl 2, knit 4 through the front legs* repeat from * to * before the edge stitch, purl 2.

Repeat rows: 1-2.

Bind off as follows: After the last row 2, turn your work over. The Front Side: slip all the stitches from the left needle to the right one; thus, the working yarn is at the end of the row, then turn your work over. The Back Side: slip 2 purlwise from the left needle to the right one, insert the left needle through the front leg of the 1st slipped stitch from left to right, and pass it over the 2nd stitch (now there is 1 stitch on the right needle) *slip 1 purlwise from the left needle to the right one, insert the left needle through the front leg of the 1st stitch on the right needle from left to right and pass it over the 2nd stitch, now there is 1 stitch on the right needle* repeat from * to * until the end of the row.

Note: For trimming, bind off using larger needles than the working ones to create a larger chain of edge stitches, as this method of binding off creates a tight chain of edge stitches.

Pattern 44

Horizontal ribbing

Reversible

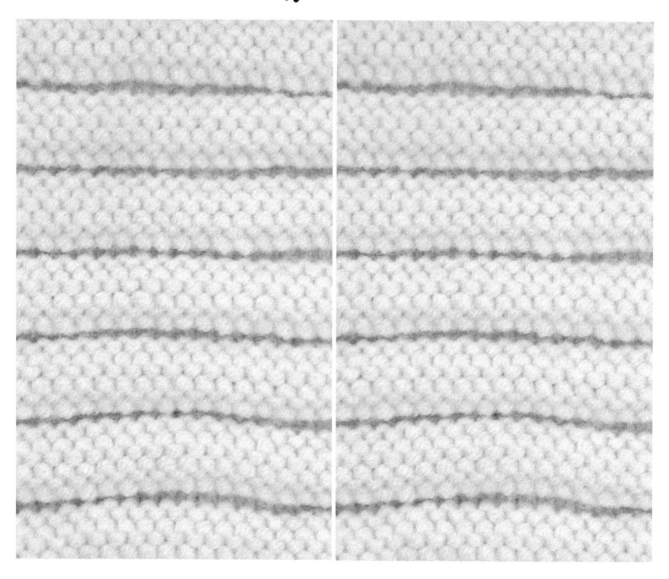

The Front Side   **The Back Side**

Cast on any number of stitches, plus 2 edge stitches. Repeat rows: 1-8.

The edge stitches are not included in the description below and must be added. Slip the first edge stitch, purl the last one.

Knit through the back leg, purl as follows: with the working yarn in front of the stitch, insert the right needle through the stitch from back to front, move the working yarn under the right needle, and pull it with the needle through the stitch. **Note:** The purl stitch that is worked this way sets up the knit stitch to be knitted through the back leg.

Description:

Row 1: Knit all the stitches through the back legs.

Row 2: Purl all the stitches.

Row 3: Purl all the stitches, turning the legs of each stitch as follows: insert the right needle through the stitch from back to front and slip it onto the right needle, then return the stitch onto the left needle and purl it.

Rows 4, 6, and 7: Repeat row 1.

Rows 5 and 8: Repeat row 2.

Repeat rows: 1-8.

Bind off after the last row 8 as follows: Slip the edge stitch onto the right needle, knit the next 1, then insert the left needle through the slipped edge stitch from left to right and pass it over the knitted one, *now there is 1 stitch on the right needle, knit the next stitch, insert the left needle through the 1st stitch on the right needle from left to right and pass it over the 2nd stitch* repeat from * to * until the end of the row.

Pattern 45

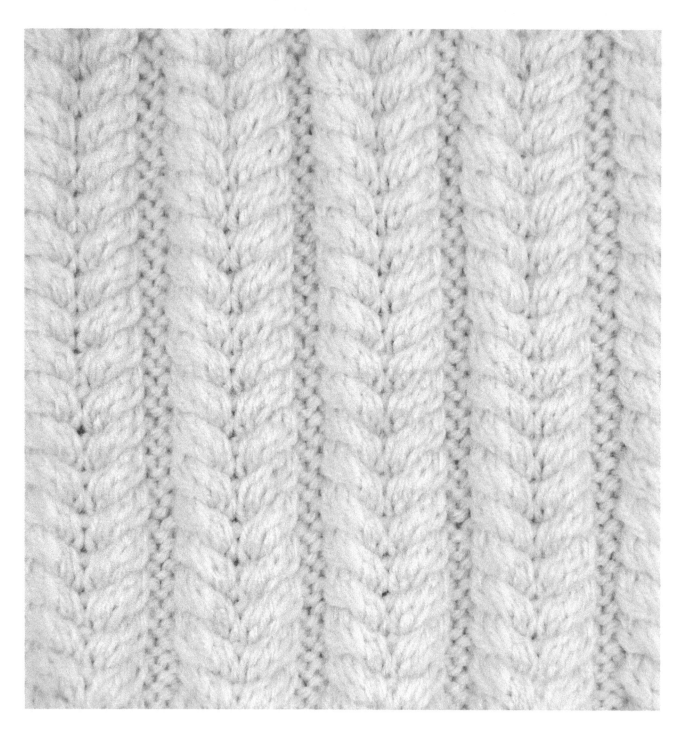

Cast on a multiple of 14, plus 2 for symmetry and 2 edge stitches. Fourteen-stitch repeat. Repeat rows: 1-2. The edge stitches are not included in the description below and must be added. Slip the first edge stitch, purl the last one as if to purl in knitting through the back leg as follows: with the working yarn in front of the stitch, insert the right needle through the stitch from back to front, move the working yarn under the right needle, and pull it with the needle through the stitch.

Knit through the front leg, purl as follows: with the working yarn in front of the stitch, insert the right needle through the stitch from back to front, wrap the working yarn forward (i.e., from yourself) around the tip of the right needle, then pull it with the right needle through the stitch. **Note:** The purl stitch that is worked this way sets up the knit stitch to be knitted through the front leg.

Description:

Row 1: *Purl 2, slip 3 onto a cable needle behind your work, knit the next 3, then knit the slipped 3, slip 3 onto a cable needle in front of your work, knit the next 3, then knit the slipped 3* repeat from * to * before the edge stitch, purl 2.

Row 2: *Knit 2, purl 12* repeat from * to * before the edge stitch, knit 2.

Repeat rows: 1-2.

Bind off as follows: After the last row 1, turn your work over. The Back Side: slip all the stitches from the left needle to the right one; thus, the working yarn is at the end of the row, then turn your work over. The Front Side: slip 2 purlwise from the left needle to the right one, insert the left needle through the front leg of the 1st slipped stitch from left to right, and pass it over the 2nd stitch (now there is 1 stitch on the right needle) *slip 1 purlwise from the left needle to the right one, insert the left needle through the front leg of the 1st stitch on the right needle from left to right and pass it over the 2nd stitch, now there is 1 stitch on the right needle* repeat from * to * until the end of the row.

Note: For trimming, bind off using larger needles than the working ones to create a larger chain of edge stitches, as this method of binding off creates a tight chain of edge stitches.

Pattern 46

Cast on a multiple of 10, plus 2 for symmetry and 2 edge stitches. Ten-stitch repeat. Repeat rows: 1-4. Slip the first edge stitch; purl the last edge stitch.

Knit through the back leg; purl as follows: with the working yarn in front of the stitch, insert the right needle from back to front, move the working yarn under the right needle and pull it with the needle through the stitch. The purl stitch that is worked this way sets up the knit stitch to be knitted through the front leg. **Knit tightly.**

Description:

Row 1: *Purl 2, knit 3, purl 2, knit 3* repeat from * to * until the end of the row before the edge stitch, purl 2.

Row 2: *Knit 2, purl 3, knit 2, purl 3* repeat from * to * until the end of the row before the edge stitch, knit 2.

Row 3: *Purl 2, knit 3 together through the front legs after moving the back legs to the front as follows: insert the right needle through the 1st stitch from back to front and slip it onto the right needle, insert the right needle through the 2nd stitch from back to front and slip it onto the right needle, insert the right needle through the 3rd stitch from back to front and slip it onto the right needle, then return these 3 stitches onto the left needle, now knit 3 together through the front legs, then yarn over forward (i.e., from yourself), purl 2, yarn over forward (i.e., from yourself), knit 3 together through the back legs* repeat from * to * until the end of the row before the edge stitch, purl 2.

Row 4: *Knit 2, purl 1, yarn over backward (i.e., to yourself), purl 1, knit 2, purl 1, yarn over backward (i.e., to yourself), purl 1* repeat from * to * until the end of the row before the edge stitch, purl 2.

Repeat rows: 1-4.

Bind off through the back legs after the last row 4 as follows: slip the edge stitch onto the right needle, knit the next 1, then insert the left needle through the slipped edge stitch from left to right and pass it over the knitted stitch; *now there is 1 stitch on the right needle; knit the next 1; now there are 2 stitches on the right needle; insert the left needle through the 1st stitch on the right needle from left to right and pass it over the 2nd stitch* repeat from * to * until the end of the row.

Pattern 47

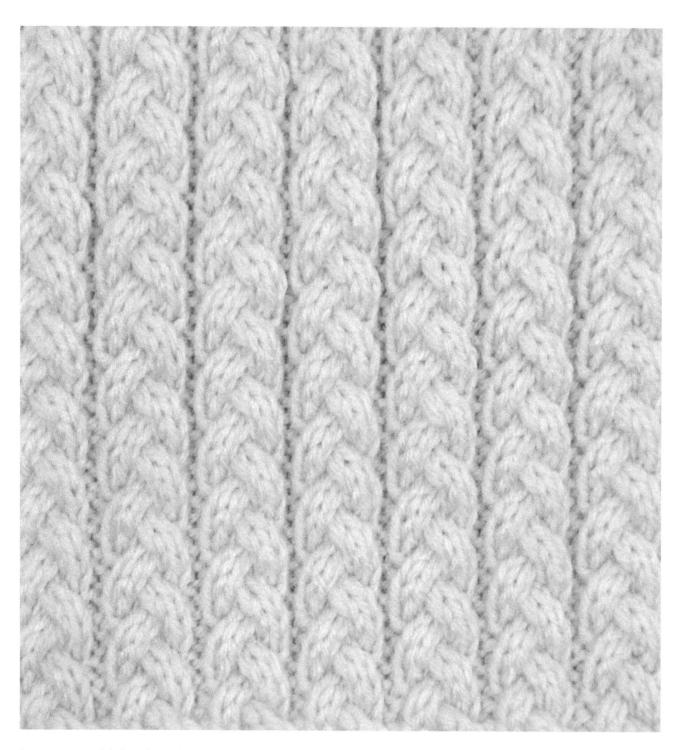

Cast on a multiple of 8, plus 2 for symmetry and 2 edge stitches. Eight-stitch repeat. Repeat rows: 1-4. The edge stitches are not included in the description below and must be added. Slip the first edge stitch, purl the last one.

Knit through the back leg, purl as follows: with the working yarn in front of the stitch, insert the right needle through the stitch from back to front, move the working yarn under the right needle, and pull it with the needle through the stitch. **Note:** The purl stitch that is worked this way sets up the knit stitch to be knitted through the back leg.

Description:

Row 1: *Purl 2, slip 2 onto a cable needle in front of your work, knit the next 2, then knit the slipped 2, knit 2* repeat from * to * until the end of the row before the edge stitch, purl 2.

Row 2: *Knit 2, purl 6* repeat from * to * until the end of the row before the edge stitch, knit 2.

Row 3: *Purl 2, knit 2, slip the next 2 onto a cable needle behind your work, knit the next 2, then knit the slipped 2* repeat from * to * until the end of the row before the edge stitch, purl 2.

Row 4: *Knit 2, purl 6* repeat from * to * until the end of the row before the edge stitch, knit 2.

Repeat rows: 1-4.

Bind off as follows: After the last row 3, turn your work over. The Back Side: slip all the stitches from the left needle to the right one; thus, the working yarn is at the end of the row, then turn your work over. The Front Side: slip 2 purlwise from the left needle to the right one, insert the left needle through the front leg of the 1st slipped stitch from left to right, and pass it over the 2nd stitch (now there is 1 stitch on the right needle) *slip 1 purlwise from the left needle to the right one, insert the left needle through the front leg of the 1st stitch on the right needle from left to right and pass it over the 2nd stitch, now there is 1 stitch on the right needle* repeat from * to * until the end of the row.

Note: For trimming, bind off using larger needles than the working ones to create a larger chain of edge stitches, as this method of binding off creates a tight chain of edge stitches.

Pattern 48

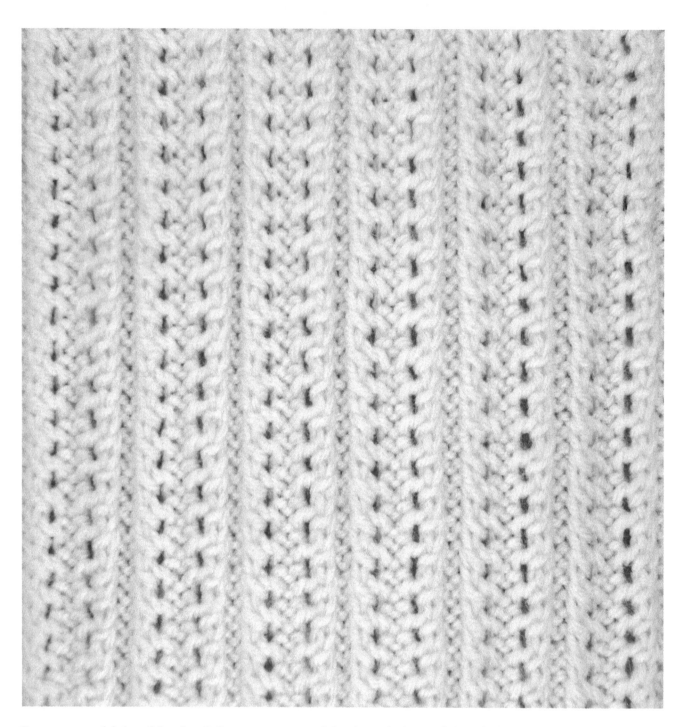

Cast on a multiple of 8, plus 2 for symmetry and 2 edge stitches. Eight-stitch repeat. Repeat rows: 1-2. The edge stitches are not included in the description below and must be added. Slip the first edge stitch, purl the last one as if to purl in knitting through the back leg as follows: with the working yarn in front of the stitch, insert the right needle through the stitch from back to front, move the working yarn under the right needle, and pull it with the needle through the stitch.

Knit through the front leg, purl as follows: with the working yarn in front of the stitch, insert the right needle through the stitch from back to front, wrap the working yarn forward (i.e., from yourself) around the tip of the right needle, then pull it with the right needle through the stitch. **Note:** The purl stitch that is worked this way sets up the knit stitch to be knitted through the front leg. **Knit tightly.**

Description:

Row 1: *Purl 2, knit 2 together through the front legs, yarn over forward (i.e., from yourself), purl 2, yarn over forward (i.e., from yourself), knit 2 together through the back legs as follows: insert the right needle through the front leg of the 1st stitch and slip it onto the right needle, then insert the right needle through the front leg of the 2nd stitch and slip it onto the right needle, then return both stitches onto the left needle, then knit 2nd together through the back legs* repeat from * to * until the end of the row before the edge stitch, purl 2.

Row 2: *Knit 2, purl 6* repeat from * to * until the end of the row before the edge stitch, knit 2.

Repeat rows: 1-2.

Bind off as follows: After the last row 2, turn your work over. The Front Side: slip all the stitches from the left needle to the right one; thus, the working yarn is at the end of the row, then turn your work over. The Back Side: slip 2 purlwise from the left needle to the right one, insert the left needle through the front leg of the 1st slipped stitch from left to right, and pass it over the 2nd stitch (now there is 1 stitch on the right needle) *slip 1 purlwise from the left needle to the right one, insert the left needle through the front leg of the 1st stitch on the right needle from left to right and pass it over the 2nd stitch, now there is 1 stitch on the right needle* repeat from * to * until the end of the row.

Note: For trimming, bind off using larger needles than the working ones to create a larger chain of edge stitches, as this method of binding off creates a tight chain of edge stitches.

Pattern 49

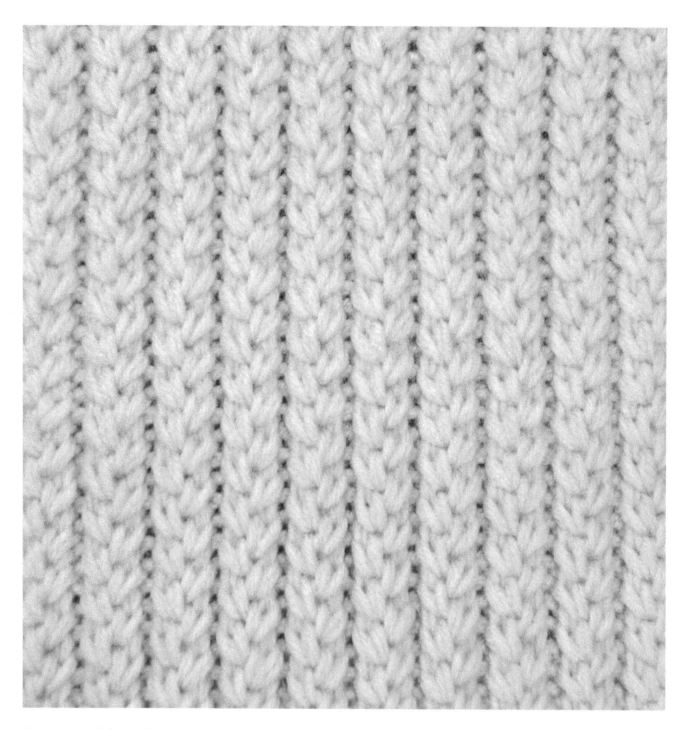

Cast on a multiple of 4, plus 1 for symmetry and 2 edge stitches. Four-stitch repeat. Repeat rows: 1-2. The edge stitches are not included in the description below and must be added. Slip the first edge stitch, purl the last one.

Knit through the back leg, purl as follows: with the working yarn in front of the stitch, insert the right needle through the stitch from back to front, then move the working yarn under the right needle and pull it with the needle through the stitch. **Note:** The purl stitch that is worked this way sets up the knit stitch to be knitted through the back leg. **Knit tightly. Use a bulky yarn.**

Description:

Row 1: *Purl 1, knit 1 through the back leg, knit the next 2 as follows: knit the 2nd stitch through the back leg, then knit the 1st stitch through the back leg* repeat from * to * until the end of the row before the edge stitch, purl 1.

Row 2: *Knit 1, purl 1, then purl the next 2 as follows: purl the 2nd stitch, then purl the 1st stitch* repeat from * to * until the end of the row before the edge stitch, knit 1.

Repeat rows: 1-2.

Bind off as follows: After the last row 2, turn your work over. The Front Side: slip all the stitches from the left needle to the right one; thus, the working yarn is at the end of the row, then turn your work over. The Back Side: slip 2 purlwise from the left needle to the right one, insert the left needle through the front leg of the 1st slipped stitch from left to right, and pass it over the 2nd stitch (now there is 1 stitch on the right needle) *slip 1 purlwise from the left needle to the right one, insert the left needle through the front leg of the 1st stitch on the right needle from left to right and pass it over the 2nd stitch, now there is 1 stitch on the right needle* repeat from * to * until the end of the row.

Note: For trimming, bind off using larger needles than the working ones to create a larger chain of edge stitches, as this method of binding off creates a tight chain of edge stitches.

Pattern 50

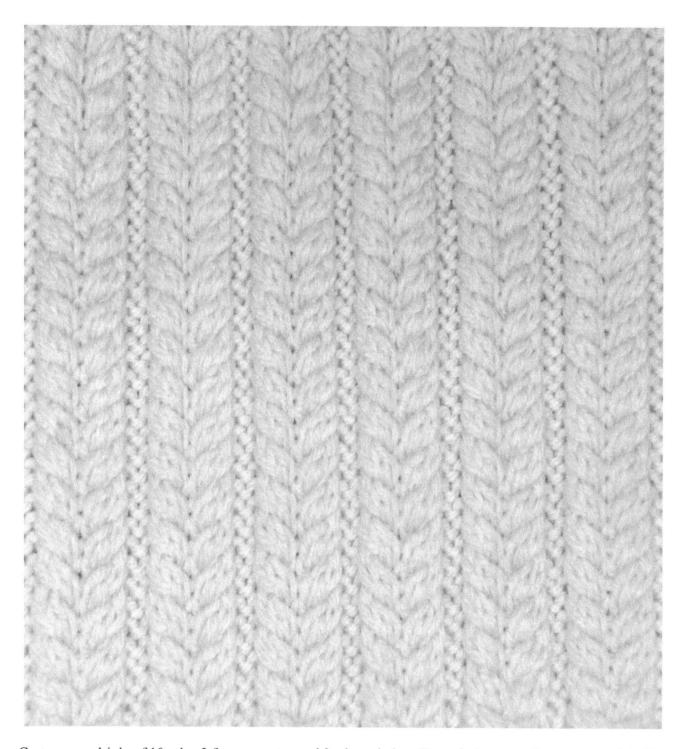

Cast on a multiple of 10, plus 2 for symmetry and 2 edge stitches. Ten-stitch repeat. Repeat rows: 1-2. The edge stitches are not included in the description below and must be added. Slip the first edge stitch, purl the last one.

Knit through the back leg, purl as follows: with the working yarn in front of the stitch, insert the right needle through the stitch from back to front, move the working yarn under the right needle, and pull it with the needle through the stitch. **Note:** The purl stitch that is worked this way sets up the knit stitch to be knitted through the back leg.

Description:

Row 1: *Purl 2, slip 2 onto a cable needle behind your work, knit the next 2, then knit the slipped 2, slip 2 onto a cable needle in front of your work, knit the next 2, then knit the slipped 2* repeat from * to * until the end of the row before the edge stitch, purl 2.

Row 2: *Knit 2, purl 8* repeat from * to * until the end of the row before the edge stitch, knit 2.

Repeat rows: 1-2.

Bind off as follows: After the last row 1, turn your work over. The Back Side: slip all the stitches from the left needle to the right one; thus, the working yarn is at the end of the row, then turn your work over. The Front Side: slip 2 purlwise from the left needle to the right one, insert the left needle through the front leg of the 1st slipped stitch from left to right, and pass it over the 2nd stitch (now there is 1 stitch on the right needle) *slip 1 purlwise from the left needle to the right one, insert the left needle through the front leg of the 1st stitch on the right needle from left to right and pass it over the 2nd stitch, now there is 1 stitch on the right needle* repeat from * to * until the end of the row.

Note: For trimming, bind off using larger needles than the working ones to create a larger chain of edge stitches, as this method of binding off creates a tight chain of edge stitches.

About the Author

Internationally recognized hand knitwear designer Marina Molo has taught various hand knitting aspects over the past 30 years. In her book, 50 Shades of Stitches, Marina Molo brings to life, in print, the most popular knitting patterns for all those who want to explore designing their knitwear.

Visit the author's online store for unique items with knit prints, including tank tops, leggings, tote bags, iPhone cases, passport holders, luggage tags, wrapping paper, ribbons, pattern folders & much more at https://www.zazzle.com/store/shades_of_stitches or scan the QR code below.

Marina Molo is currently working on several new publishing projects with SCR Media Inc.

What Do You Think of 50 Shades of Stitches?

*First of all, thank you for purchasing this book, **50 Shades of Stitches Volume 1.***

I know you could have picked any other books to read, but you chose this book, and for that, I am incredibly grateful. I hope that it adds value and quality to your everyday life.

If you like this book and found it helpful, I'd like to hear from you and hope that you could take some time to post a review on Amazon. Your feedback and support will help the author to improve her writing craft significantly for future projects and make this book even better. Just type this link into your web browser Getbook.at/Vol1 or scan the code below

*I want you, the reader, to know that your review is critical and so, please **leave a review.** All you have to do is type into your web browser **Getbook.at/Vol1** or scan the QR code above*

I wish you all the best in your future success!

Lightning Source UK Ltd.
Milton Keynes UK
UKHW032241060223
416580UK00007B/708